THE FLIGHT OF THE DALAI LAMA

By the same author

Autobiography

FIRES OF SPRING

STRANGERS IN THE SUN

Travel

THE WHITE DESERT

TRANS-SIBERIAN

CITIES (with Rupert Croft-Cooke)

DISTANT PLACES

Politics

HOW STRONG IS AMERICA?

THE MENACE OF JAPAN

War

A HANDFUL OF ASHES

PRISONER OF WAR

HITLER'S LAST HOPE (with Ernest Phillips)

General

NEWSPAPER REPORTING

THE FLIGHT
OF
THE DALAI LAMA

by

NOEL BARBER

LONDON
HODDER & STOUGHTON

Made and printed in Great Britain for
Hodder and Stoughton Limited London
by Cox & Wyman Limited London
Fakenham and Reading

For
RALPH IZZARD
and
JOHN MOULT
With my grateful thanks

AUTHOR'S NOTE

This book is the record of events in Tibet up to the time I completed the manuscript last year, and the views expressed are based on the situation as it then stood. Subsequently events have marched with swiftness, but they confirm rather than alter, the opinions here expressed.

CONTENTS

ILLUSTRATIONS

[1] Associated Newspapers Ltd.
[2] Camera Press Ltd.
[3] D. I. Macdonald
[4] Lt. Col. L. S. Fenton
[5] The Associated Press Ltd.
[6] Planet News Ltd.
[7] P. A. Reuter Photos Ltd.
[8] Paris Match

MAPS

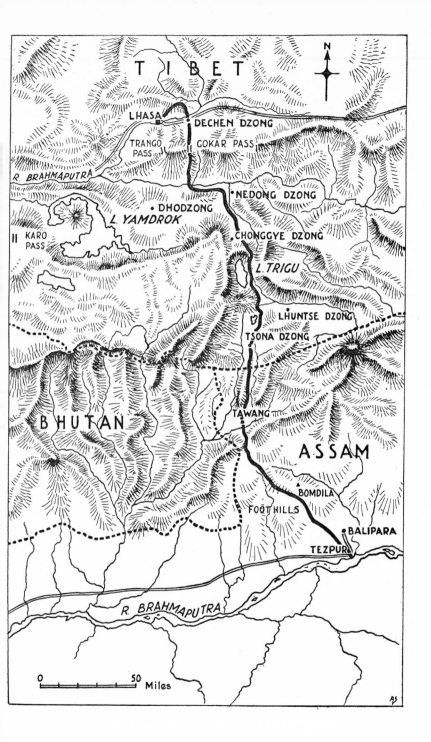

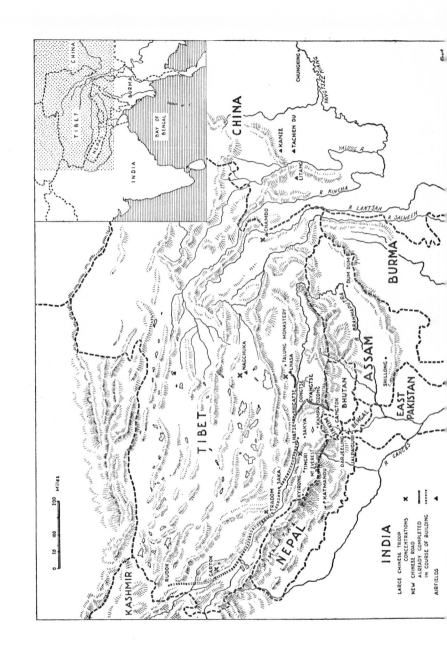

I

WELCOME IN TEZPUR

Saturday, April 18, 1959, dawned bright and clear after a night of violent thunderstorms, and within an hour a hot sun had dried the small world of Tezpur in Assam; the pools had vanished from its brown dusty streets, and in the green tea gardens that spread towards the mountains the long lines of pickers were soon at work.

This was the day (and I doubt if there will ever be another one like it in Tezpur) when the entire township was suffused by the presence of one man, the Dalai Lama, as he reached the climax of a long and dangerous journey. In a world grown cynical, it was at first hard to realise the impression of awe, reverence and mysticism that this gentle lonely man evoked as he walked amidst the crowds. There were not only Buddhists, but the men and women of many other religions, including Christians like myself, yet I cannot remember ever being so moved, despite the fact that I found it hard to believe this young man was the living reincarnation of a Saint who lived centuries ago and not merely the son of a poor peasant who had been elected to his high office by a series of tests that no man with any pretence to rational thinking could ever accept. Yet there it was. When he reached Tezpur, I was standing with Heinrich Harrer, the author of *Seven Years in Tibet* and who could be excused for being visibly touched. Then "Heinig"—honest and one of the least assuming men in the world—turned to me with tears in his eyes and said in his Austrian accent, "So, Noel, you too feel what I feel?" and I realised there were tears in my eyes as well.

To millions the Dalai Lama was and is both king and God, and so to millions who had worshipped him while he lived so far away in Lhasa, and who had never thought to set eyes on him, it was as though God had come down to the plains and was now walking amongst them. From the moment he arrived at Foothills shortly after seven in the morning, to the minute his train pulled out of Tezpur's tiny station shortly after one o'clock, his presence was everywhere. It was a very moving experience.

Behind it, overshadowing it, there was of course the past and the future. Who could watch the triumphant yet intensely pathetic spectacle of his arrival without wondering about its effect on his isolated country and the millions of Buddhists in the world? It was not the multitude acclaiming him, nor the presence of the Dalai Lama himself that alone was so touching. It was accentuated by deeper, more funda-mental analytical thoughts that insisted on crowding one's emotions and posing the question "What next?" in the life of this peasant grown wise beyond his years, and "What next?" in the dsetinies of his uncowed people.

What next indeed, I wondered, as very slowly the Dalai Lama ascended the red-carpeted steps to the throne with, a step behind him, a retainer holding a golden parasol to shade his head from the sun. At this moment, at the end of this magnificent journey of escape, as the Dalai Lama, with his utterly serene smile, blessed the crowd, I knew I was witness to the turning of a page in the history of Tibet. Now, in this dusty, unkempt, straggling town of Tezpur, another king, this time a king of the heavens, had joined the long list of exiled monarchs driven from their countries by the forces of oppression. Once again, it seemed, might had triumphed over right, so that this day of rejoicing became a strange mixture of divine beauty and desperate pathos.

I have never in all my life seen a man with a more beautiful smile than the Dalai Lama's, the smile of a child who has not yet lost faith in humanity, or perhaps the smile of a very saintly man. Ever since I first became interested in Tibet's struggle against the Chinese I had wanted to meet him; I had read much of him before, especially in Heinig's fascinat-ing book; and then I had been much impressed with the accounts of him given to me by the Tibetans I had met at Kalimpong and also when I trekked across the Himalayas to the frontier. I remember I visited the house of some rich Buddhists who lived on the road between Kalimpong and Gangtok, the capital of Sikkim. My hostess was a wise old lady, still beautiful, much travelled and fascinated by English gardening which she practised assiduously in that arduous climate. She was half Tibetan, and her daughter, equally beautiful, had the pink cheeks and high cheekbones of Tibet. Once (on his previous visit to India) the Dalai Lama had stayed at their house, where they lived in some opulence, and there too as we stood in the golden chapel dedicated to his memory, I had been immensely impressed with the tenderness, as well as the reverence, with which these devout Buddhists spoke of him and his days of rest there.

As I saw him now at close quarters, I realised how well worth while had been my long journey, for I had flown from Equatorial Africa, for this one morning of my life; an emotion sharpened by the knowledge that behind his smile and gentleness, there was no road back for the God-king of Buddhism. He too must have known that his public condemnation of Red China on this day would make the masters of Asia his implacable enemies for life.

It made no difference to the evil powers that had caused his flight that he was a divine king as well as a political ruler, and God, if it comes to that, to many of the Chinese who still secretly believe in the spiritual values of Buddhism rather than the more materialistic doctrines of the Chinese Communist Party. When the Dalai Lama set foot on Indian soil and started the long trek down from Tawang to Bomdila, and then to Tezpur to catch the train to the hill station above New Delhi, a decisive turning-point in the history of Tibet had been reached. The flight of the Dalai Lama does not mean the end of Tibet as we know it, for this unhappy country, whose only desire is to be left alone to practise its faith, has suffered oppression before in its long history, and risen above it. Its wars with China have been an integral part of its daily life, and it has remained steadfast to its beliefs, wrapped in its own particular brand of courage, and has always risen again.

But now, the last day of the Dalai Lama's journey—and the last day in a phase of Tibet's history—had arrived and it turned out to be an incredible mixture of religion, politics and the workaday world. In much the same way as devout Catholics unashamedly chatter in their churches (and are none the worse for that) so this historic occasion at Tezpur was seized as an excuse for outings by entire families who not only came to be blessed in the grounds of the local college, but who wanted to have a good time with plenty of fun for the kiddies in a large open space where access was normally denied to them.

The Indians arrived in their thousands, and in everything from American station wagons (from which they served cold chicken lunches in Western style picnic baskets) to rickshaws. At times the scene looked like an English point-to-point meeting; at others like an Oriental version of an evangelist campaign; and at others, in the still moments in the hot air, it was something again, beautiful and touching and simple and unforgettable.

In the centre of the college grounds the throne had been erected with red linen serving as a carpet for the steps leading up to it. The throne itself was surmounted with a conical thatched roof lined in scarlet material, with a large inscription worked into the underneath of the roof under which the Dalai Lama stood. On this dais, perhaps twenty feet high, stood a wooden chair of the kitchen variety, a table with a gaudy cloth on it, three bowls of flowers, a golden urn, and a battery of microphones with which the Dalai Lama seemed quite at home. Below were two rows of chairs for the party that had fled with him from Tibet, noblemen with braided pigtails wound round their heads, and turquoise earrings four inches long in their left ears.

Roped off by bamboo fences, the white paint not yet dry, ten thousand Indians and Tibetans were massed under a sea of black umbrellas—the umbrellas that every Indian in

The author on the way to Tibet

The Potala palace, Lhasa

Assam carries at that time of the year as a protection either against the hot sun or the sudden storms. To open the proceedings the mayor of Tezpur made a speech, commendably brief and copies of which had been distributed by the local garages the night before, a precaution well advised since nobody could hear what he said due to the chatter on the throne while the mayor spoke.

The people on the dais disregarded this minor official completely, and kept on whispering to the Dalai Lama who took no notice either and indeed at one moment was seen to give a wide, boyish grin at some private joke. Though we had been told that the Dalai Lama would remain alone on the throne when he spoke, this was not to be, for the local Indian leaders refused to relinquish their brief place in the sun even when the Dalai Lama was presented with a white scarf and when he blessed the crowd, which he did by leaning over the edge of the throne and scattering in the hot wind a handful of lotus blossoms. He alone of the motley assembly on the throne preserved his dignity, perhaps by instinctively ignoring the hangers-on and smiling to the lookers-on.

All day the Dalai Lama wore the same russet-brown robe with a touch of yellow at the throat, white socks, modern shoes, and a small highly embroidered Tibetan apron round his waist. His hair was close cropped and he drove up in a red American car in which he had left a small attaché case (very much like a man carrying with him his masonic regalia) and two felt hats on the shelf behind the back seat, the hats stuck one on top of the other as they often are in Tibet. The car bore the Indian flag over one mudguard and his personal flag, with rising suns on it, over the other, both the flags tied to split bamboos and fastened to the car bumpers with bits of old wire.

In this car he drove along the road to the college grounds, the three miles lined with crowds, including hundreds of schoolgirls in white saris edged in scarlet, almost like uniforms, and looking very beautiful. Others had their long, shining pigtails intertwined with red wool and long,

B

dangling ornaments of gold hanging half-way down their backs from their tresses. Local police in red turbans kept order (or tried to) in a traffic chaos that included everything from men on crutches to men on decorated lumbering elephants hired out at ten rupees an hour for the rich who wanted their religion the comfortable way and with an unimpeded view. At the entrance to the college grounds a triumphal arch had been erected of white linen stretched across a great bamboo frame thirty feet high (to give plenty of room for the elephants) and from one grass verge to the other. It was liberally decorated with hundreds of coloured saucer-shaped hats.

The cars roared along, the mayor made his speech, the Dalai Lama blessed the crowd, and in twenty minutes it was all over, and as I walked off the field with its football pitches, schoolkids were already punting a ball about, and a score of ancient Indians were clearing up sweet papers, orange peel, banana skins and other litter, the inevitable sign that any outdoor meeting has been successful.

The blessing of the multitude in the college grounds was the most dramatic moment of the day, but the most touching was when the Dalai Lama reached Foothills early in the morning. Foothills was the small village on the "free" side of NEFA (North-Eastern Frontier Agency), to which all access was prohibited, and therefore in theory anybody who wanted to go to Foothills to meet the Dalai Lama could do so merely by hiring a car and driving along a public highway. However, as the time approached for the Dalai Lama's arrival, the Indian Government announced that nobody would be allowed to travel to Foothills by the only serviceable road, either on the day before his arrival or the Saturday. The excuse offered was that the rains had made the bridges unsafe for "so many cars". It was a typical political excuse, one of the many devised by the Indians to keep the Dalai Lama away from the Press, and completely untrue as we were to see for ourselves when the ban was rescinded and we were able to use the road.

At Foothills, the journey of a month across the mountains

can really be said to have ended, and ended at the precise
moment when the Dalai Lama climbed stiffly from his jeep
and walked across a "red carpet" of 120 groundsheets laid
down by the men of the Assam Rifles. The party clambered
out, stretched in the hot dawn; tired, stiff, a little bewildered,
the ninety of them then trudged across those army groundsheets from one world to another, with the morning steam
already rising in wraiths above the jungle. Assamese troops
guarded the party with fixed bayonets, forming a cordon
with only three feet between each man, as the men, women
and one child walked to a thatched bungalow set in a garden
alive with banana, peach and custard apple trees.

Here they breakfasted in the early morning heat and I
wondered during the period of waiting what this august
party would consider suitable food for starting off such an
important day (my previous experience of Tibetans indicated that a bowl of rice or champa would be enough).
But not at all. The entire party sat down to a typically
English breakfast of cornflakes, poached eggs, toast and
marmalade, with coffee or tea (Indian), and as in any party
that included children, the biggest breakfast was eaten by
the youngest member, the Dalai Lama's thirteen-year-old
brother, a rosy-cheeked youngster with twinkling eyes, and
dressed in a brown gown with tiny fur-lined boots. Like his
elder brother, he is also a living Buddha, but his spiritual
office did not prevent him from munching his way steadily
through two plates of cornflakes and a double portion of
eggs.

Just after breakfast, suddenly and without warning, one of
the noblemen of the Dalai Lama's party gave a cry of
delight, broke through the military guard, pushed past a
flabbergasted major of the Assam Rifles, grabbed hold of
Heinig Harrer and rushed him to the Dalai Lama's mother,
who was obviously delighted to see him again. The Dalai
Lama was watching, and when he saw who it was, his face
broke into an enormous happy smile. But this was India,
and, as Harrer was to find later at Mussoorie, the Indians did
everything in their power to stop the Dalai Lama or any of

his entourage from speaking to Harrer, so anxious were they that no "anti-Chinese" stories should gain world circulation.

From Foothills the Dalai Lama travelled to Tezpur's "Circuit House", a V.I.P. bungalow perched on a hill above the Brahmaputra. He looked remarkably fresh and cheerful as he drove into the town, passing under a scarlet banner "Welcome Tezpur Municipality" and with hundreds of police struggling in vain to keep India's sacred cows, plus an assortment of goats and water buffalo, off the thirty-mile road along which these animals have from time immemorial been accustomed to force traffic to a standstill. Other police were striving to keep cattle off the single-track railway along which the Dalai Lama was to travel within a few hours.

At the Circuit House, the Dalai Lama stopped for yet another ceremonial cup of tea (with, I noticed, a few refreshing oranges sneaked in). The Master of Tea, one of the three Lord Attendants who travelled the entire way with him, supervised the tea drinking in conjunction with an Indian chef. For an hour and a half the Circuit House was in wild confusion. Normally nothing happens at this placid building on the edge of Tezpur, with its lawns neatly fenced off in white like paddocks, and clouds of butterflies and mynah birds giving the movement and noise of a modern ballet. But on this day scores of Tibetans jostled for position to see their leader arrive with the retinue that had made the journey with him. Technicians by the dozen trampled the green grass as they set up batteries of microphones and television cameras. Assamese officers, English to the last swagger cane, strutted around getting in each other's way and rehearsing their troops in a "Present Arms".

It was here that the Dalai Lama's statement damning Red China was released to the world. It was a thorough, restrained document, tracing the record of China's broken promises since the invasion of Tibet. Officials insisted that the Dalai Lama had written it himself, but though I believe he wrote that part of it dealing with the Chinese invasion, I thought I detected the hand of an Indian official in the section devoted to eulogising India as the perfect host. This statement was not read by the Dalai Lama but by a senior official of the court, who droned it out in Tibetan for the benefit of radio and television reporters, and a translation was then read out by a junior official. The text of this statement is given in a later chapter.

Ironically, at the very time that the Dalai Lama's attack on Red China was being read, broadcast and televised on the lawns of Tezpur's Circuit House, Chou En-lai in Peking was reporting to the National People's Congress, "Although the Dalai Lama has been abducted to India, we still hope he will be able to free himself from the hold of the rebels and return to the motherland."

What inept asses these Communists can be! And what ridiculous liars—to make such a statement (even if mainly for internal consumption) when 10,000 people, including a hundred journalists, could see for themselves on this historic day, and tell the world, of the look of happiness on the Dalai Lama's face.

II

MOTIVES AND REACTIONS

This story started and will end with a moment of destiny. Sometimes in the history of a country it is possible to seize on a particular instant or episode so dramatic that, though it passes swiftly, it crystallises for all the world to see a turning-point in that country's fortunes. Much may have happened before, and the future still has to be lived, but it is on the moment of drama that the world's attention is focused.

Such an instance I described in the previous chapter, but this story, which tells of the Dalai Lama's escape, will do more than that, I hope, for it is not only the moment of destiny that is important; so are the events that shape such a moment, and it happened that before the Dalai Lama fled from Tibet, I was able to see just what those events were. The story is a long and tangled one that took me not only to Tezpur to welcome the God-king, but up through the high passes of the Himalayas to talk, myself, with the leaders of the Tibetan guerrillas and so piece together the complete story of what was happening, and how it led to the great revolt at Lhasa, and the escape of the Dalai Lama.

One or two important points should be borne in mind at the outset.

Firstly, it is wrong to suppose that the Dalai Lama fled from Tibet only because he was in peril of his life. It is true that his court at Lhasa did believe his life to be in danger, and urged him to flee and that he agreed to their advice. But many of those who escaped with him insist that he did not fly to India merely for religious sanctuary, for he could quite easily and quite safely have remained in southern Tibet surrounded by loyal Khambas, with an easy outlet to India if the position worsened. I believe that his purpose in travelling to India instead of remaining in southern Tibet was to appeal to the Indian Government or perhaps even personally to the United Nations and I am not alone in thinking thus.

Among the many friends like Heinig who helped me, I count high a bearded, jovial, Tibetan-speaking missionary called George Patterson who lives at Darjeeling, and who was of the greatest assistance to me in planning my trek over the mountains a few months before the Dalai Lama's escape, and who later flew to Tezpur and shared the same tea planter's bungalow with me as we awaited the Dalai Lama's arrival. George knew the Dalai Lama, and like a good Christian he had an unwavering hatred for the Communist Chinese, and had written several books and also some remarkable despatches to *The Daily Telegraph*, about Tibet; and he had this to say:

"According to knowledgeable Tibetan sources he is no religious exile fleeing to some safe retreat to receive permitted homage from a few exiles and refugees, but a God-king of a proud, angry, and courageous people coming to demand moral recognition and help in the name of religion from those who profess to believe in it against the forces of materialism." (*The Daily Telegraph*, April 15, 1959.)

Secondly, it is equally important to remember that the Dalai Lama was unfortunately very wrong if he supposed that his appearance in India would guarantee him even moral help; and in fact his flight might never have been necessary had Nehru given him a little moral support a little earlier. Though the role of the Chinese Government has been wicked beyond belief in its war of extermination against Tibet, there may be some who believe India to be just as culpable, for who is to determine which is the most despicable, the bully or the hypocrite?

When the Dalai Lama finally reached Mussoorie, he was made a virtual prisoner. The main motive behind his arrival in India—to present his case to the world—was ruthlessly prohibited by Nehru who put up a fourteen-foot barbed-wire fence round his bungalow and refused to permit any visitors to see the Dalai Lama or his court. It is quite obvious that a man who is God to millions of people cannot himself walk to the gates and invite people to come and see him, and unless people request audiences with him, nothing can be done. No requests ever reached him. This Nehru knew, and even though later the Dalai Lama was to receive the Press, that makes no difference, for the value of any plea made by the Dalai Lama rested on that plea being made quickly, immediately after his dramatic escape and while the entire world, even if it could do nothing, was actively sympathetic to the plight of Tibet.

Nehru knows that human memory is short, and that in the swiftly moving world of today, one tragedy is soon overshadowed by another. He deliberately refused the Dalai Lama permission to state his case to the world while the situation was critical, he deliberately banned him from any contact with people who might have assisted him or Tibet at the most vital moment, and what is even worse, he acted thus by hypocritically and falsely misrepresenting the entire Chinese–Tibet case.

It is only natural that successive régimes in China have sedulously fostered the belief that Tibet had always agreed to Chinese suzerainty in one form or another, for China has wanted physical domination over Tibet since early in the eighteenth century. But in actual fact since the Tibetans threw the Chinese out of Tibet in 1912, the Tibetans have always managed their own affairs, agreeing only (after persuasion by the British) to Chinese suzerainty providing it was limited to the formal suzerainty that had existed under the Manchus. Nehru's wickedest lie is that he has unwaveringly pretended to the world that this agreement on Chinese suzerainty was unconditional, and that it had been agreed to by both the British and the Tibetans at the Tripartite conference at Simla in 1914. That is absolutely untrue. It was not unconditional. At that conference, Tibet made no concessions to the Chinese, and only agreed to a direct treaty between Britain and Tibet in which we never sought more than a sphere of influence in Tibet.

As Mr. Hugh Richardson, the last British representative in Tibet, who left the country in 1950, says, "Mr. Nehru has consistently disregarded the facts by speaking as though there had been an unconditional admission of Chinese suzerainty both by the Tibetans and the British Government whose responsibilities he had assumed. This was an unwarranted depreciation of Tibet's actual position and made it plain to China from the outset that India would give little support to Tibet. The new situation was not only accepted with alacrity, it was fulsomely justified in a treaty between India and China in 1954.

"Mr. Nehru must surely know that, whatever was 'the general opinion' about China's suzerainty over Tibet, there was not a trace of actual Chinese authority there after 1912. He must know that in 1950 the Chinese invaded a country inhabited by a non-Chinese people who had undeniably managed all their own affairs for thirty-eight years and that they imposed an agreement on them by force. That action is what Mr. Nehru has recently described as 'legal'; and on that basis, rigid and unseeing, he described the tragic happenings at Lhasa as China's internal affair." (*The Manchester Guardian*, April 5, 1959.)

By the time the Dalai Lama reached Tezpur on that hot Saturday in April, India had already arranged for his comfort in an old bungalow at Mussoorie, where, as I say, he and his family were caged in a small enclosure surrounded by a barbed-wire fence. It was a sorry ending to such an epic march.

Thirdly, it must never be forgotten that there is a fundamental difference between the earlier attacks on Tibet and the present Chinese invasion. In the past Chinese aggression was never as total as it is today. On many occasions the Chinese warlords were fighting among themselves; Tibet was a side issue to greater issues, and the sporadic invasions by the Chinese were rarely made in strength. Today, nobody but a fool can deny that the new Red China is as solidly totalitarian as Soviet Russia. Its aims are as ruthless—world domination. There is no possibility, in the foreseeable future anyway, of a revolt within China. It is ruled by a fist of iron not even masked by a velvet glove. Its millions of peasants are robots. This in turn means that, again in the foreseeable future, there is no hope of any change in the present conflict in Tibet, except a change for the worse.

The Khambas may still fight the Chinese when they can, but without the divine inspiration of a God in their midst, I doubt if they will continue for long as valiantly as in the immediate past. Indeed, for a long time to come, Tibet will be wrapped in a shroud of silence and we shall know little or nothing of what is happening behind its mountainous borders.

For me, as I jostled with the Tibetans at Tezpur, I was watching the climax of a great drama, the moment of no return; but then for me this was a very personal experience, for though I am no Tibetologist like Heinig or George Patterson, I had in my own small way contributed a little to the meagre public information about Chinese activities in Tibet, particularly in the months preceding the flight of the Dalai Lama.

By good fortune I had met many guerrillas on the Tibetan border and learned at first-hand the valiant fight they were making against such terrible odds. In a way, therefore, the arrival of the Dalai Lama at Tezpur was a natural climax to my earlier interest in the unknown facts about the Khamba revolt. So it was that when the Dalai's party arrived and I smelled again the odour of rancid butter—not unpleasant when one is used to it—I was whisked back in time to the exciting days when I climbed across the Himalayas to try and find something of the truth about the hidden war in Tibet. Then I was in at the beginning. Now, it was as though I had returned to see the last episode in a terrible and true story.

For many years to come Tibet will be hidden behind a curtain more severe than any the Tibetans themselves tried to erect against the outside world; a curtain made in Communist China; and I fear she can expect no help from the outside world.

This was the ominous, ever-present shadow behind the drama of the Dalai Lama's escape; this was what made it a moment of history and not just a mere adventure story. But the flight from the summer palace in Tibet was no sudden plan. It was the culmination of a long series of events in the life of Tibet, in the lives of its strange Buddhist Lamas, with their mixture of the true faith and mumbo-jumbo. And before one looks at those events, it might be as well to go back to the beginning of Tibet to see how it embraced Buddhism, how a small child was chosen as the present Dalai Lama, and then to the Chinese invasion which was to lead to the escape story that is the theme of this volume.

III

THE GROWTH OF RELIGION IN TIBET

Before the seventh century, Tibet did not exist as a country. Its barren storm-swept plateaux, jagged peaks and narrow valleys were peopled only by scattered tribes, each holding jealously to its own small parcel of territory and waging a sporadic kind of clan warfare against its neighbours in the next valley. There were no towns, no roads, no government, no rulers other than the hundreds of petty chieftains, until about A.D. 630. It is impossible to be exact about the date, since there is no written history of Tibet at that time, but about then a remarkable man emerged to weld the country together.

His name was Songtsen Gompo; a tribal leader like the others, but who was capable of fighting and beating his neighbours. History throws up men like this from time to time, and they invariably follow a familiar pattern. They are men who can turn a rabble into a disciplined force and then use that force to conquer and absorb, then conquer again. One by one the tribes fell under his rule. Some he fought, some threw in their lot with him without a struggle, but the result was inevitable. By the time he was twenty-five Songtsen Gompo was the first ruler of "united Tibet"—and more. He had looked over the rim of his land-locked kingdom, and conquered a large part of northern Burma, a piece of Nepal and a slice of western China. And, perhaps with the instinctive knowledge that alliances by marriage make frontiers safer than any army can, he also acquired two wives, one a young Chinese princess, the other from the royal family of Nepal.

Up to this time there had been little in the way of recognised religion among the Tibetans, though ironically anticipating Darwin by more than a thousand years, the tribal ancients believed the Tibetans came from monkey ancestors. The legend told how a monkey more wise than his fellows came down from the trees and made a fortuitous marriage with a goddess of the mountains; how he took their off-spring, seven in number, back to the forest; how they grew in numbers and intelligence and came down from the trees to walk on the ground, to till the soil and herd animals, and become the first men of Tibet.

If Songtsen Gompo had any religion it was based on legends like this; a crude animistic mixture of nature worship, witchcraft and fear, called Bon Po. But the two young princesses, as well as sharing a common husband, shared a common religion. They were devout Buddhists, and with little effort they persuaded Songtsen Gompo over to at least an outward acceptance of their faith, until eventually he decided that, as well as having one ruler, Tibet would now have one religion, the faith of Gautama, the Buddha, the Enlightened One.

This was the golden age in Tibet. From China, in the wake of their princess, came an army of skilled craftsmen—builders, masons, carpenters, weavers, men cunning in the art of ceramics. From India came scholars and teachers. A Tibetan alphabet was contrived based on Sanskrit, and the sacred writings of the Indian Buddhists were translated and spread among the warriors and herdsmen.

The great monasteries, destined to shape the fate of the country for centuries ahead, were founded and culture marched alongside military might in the growth of the new country. As kings were born and died, Tibet ruthlessly stamped out any signs of rebellion in her empire; and as late as A.D. 741, during the reign of Tihtsong Detsen, the Chinese were still paying a yearly tribute of 50,000 pieces of silken brocade to keep the peace. In 755 they tried to stop the annual payment but the Tibetan warriors poured over the frontier, conquered a slice of China as far east as the Shensi province border, and forced the Chinese emperor into hiding. These sporadic border wars continued until about a hundred years later when a boundary treaty was signed at Chorten Karpo and the actual White Chorten which has given the place its name still stands today.

It was not the kind of treaty that could be torn up like today's international scraps of paper. The details were engraved on three great pillars of stone in Chinese and Tibetan characters. One today is preserved in Lhasa, another is at Sien in the Shensi province and the third is at Chorten Karpo itself.

With men like Songtsen Gompo and Tihtsong Detsen on the throne to keep the warlike clansmen in check, Tibet prospered. But men of that calibre are rare and the task was too much for their successors. Geography itself worked against them. A land of isolated valleys and almost impassable mountains is not easy to control even in the twentieth century. The power and energy of the succession of lay-kings dwindled, and as it dwindled the power of the monasteries grew, for they were the only centres where there were large concentrations of able and devoted men. Monks put aside the spiritual for the temporal.

Warriors were hired. Each monastery built up its own private army and the Lamas soon became virtual rulers of large pockets of the country, paying no more than lip service to the kings.

Three hundred years after Songtsen Gompo the end came, when Lang Dama, last of the lay-kings, failed in a final attempt to smash the power of the monasteries. His army almost gone, he contemplated flight to China, but he did not even have time to escape, for a monk disguised in black robes and (for some reason that legend fails to explain) riding a white horse blackened with soot, penetrated the court, assassinated the king and escaped in triumph to the monastery fortresses.

The old order collapsed. There were no more kings. Tribal warfare began again and from the resulting confusion the monasteries emerged as the one dominating cohesive force; and in Tibet today the Lamas still perform a New Year ritual, the Dance of the Black Hat, commemorating the un-named monk whose dagger thrust had changed the history of Tibet.

From then on, organised rule fell more and more into the hands of the monasteries and in A.D. 1244, Basba, first Lama king and leader of the Sakya or Red Hat sect, became supreme ruler.

Tibet was certainly no vassal state of China at this stage, as is shown when Basba was invited to pay a state visit to China by the ruling Khan. One version claims that his host was Kublai Khan himself; certainly this host was a descendant of the great Mongolian conqueror, Ghengis Khan, and to show his great respect, the Chinese ruler personally escorted the Lama king for the first four months of the long journey back to his mountain fortress.

With the Lamas firmly in the seat of power in the thirteenth century—a power they have never lost—this is perhaps the appropriate time to take a look at Buddhism as it is practised by some 500 million Asians, and its variant, Tibetan Lamaism.

Buddhism basically follows the Hindu belief of reincarnation. The soul, according to both Hindu and Buddhist, revolves on an endless circle of birth, death and rebirth. The body is no more than a shell or earthly vehicle and as such is of minor importance. The soul goes on round the circle, and as in the Hindu doctrine of Karma, virtuous conduct is rewarded in future reincarnations and misdeeds lead to retribution. Again, like the Hindus, a true Buddhist sees the world as a place of ignorance and sorrow from which, by devotion, he should seek escape into Nirvana, the ultimate bliss. And finally, borrowing yet again from the Hindus, a Buddhist is taught that the true way of wisdom lies in subjecting and subduing the appetites and lusts of the flesh.

Siddhastha Gautama, the Great Buddha, was born a prince in northern India in 563 B.C., and until the age of twenty-nine, says history, he lived the life of a wealthy luxury-loving princeling with a palace, a beautiful wife, and a child. One day, in defiance of his father's orders, he left the seclusion of his royal home and saw in quick succession a sick man, an old man, a corpse and a half-starved, half-crazed holy man. Shocked into realisation of the harshness of life outside the walls of his palace, he renounced wealth, family and rank and for six years, clad in saffron robes, wandered as a penniless head-shaven beggar, seeking a spiritual light, after the manner of the Hindu, through mortification of the flesh. But he found no solution in this form of self-torture and finally he sat himself down under the sacred Bodhi Tree and vowed that he would not stir until his meditations brought him the answer to the riddle of life.

For forty-nine days he sat there, resisting, says legend, the temptations of Mara the Evil One, till on the last day he achieved what he was seeking. From that day he became known as "the Buddha", which simply means "the enlightened one".

Having reached this lofty plane he could, according to Buddhist teachings, have at once left his mortal body for the last time and passed into Nirvana, but such a departure would have conflicted with his own convictions. Buddhism, as its founder saw it, must be essentially a gentle humanist religion.

Instead he remained on earth, preaching his faith of the Four Noble Truths and the Noble Eightfold Path for forty-five years before he finally passed into Nirvana at the age of eighty.

These are the Four Noble Truths he taught in his wanderings up and down India:

1. Suffering is universal.
2. Suffering is caused by selfish desire.
3. Suffering can only be ended by eliminating desire.
4. Desire can only be eliminated by following the Middle Way as outlined in the precepts of the Eightfold Path.

And this is the Path:

1. Right knowledge.
2. Right intention.

A Korean artiste singing at a tea-party given by the Dalai Lama's mother and sister at their house in honour of women members of a Government Delegation. The fourth on the right is the Dalai Lama's sister

The Dalai Lama in a palanquin which is carried by four specially selected men

A pilgrim 'measuring his length' to Lhasa—it will take him eight months to reach there

Idol of Chenrezi (the All-Seeing-One), which has 11 heads 1,000 arms and hands; each hand has an eye in the palm

3. Right speech.
4. Right conduct.
5. Right means of livelihood.
6. Right effort.
7. Right thoughts.
8. Right concentration.

For all Buddhists, the third and fourth of these concepts are the greatest and their rather cryptic phrasing has been expanded into an everyday code of conduct known as the Five Precepts:

1. Abstain from taking life.
2. Abstain from taking what is not given.
3. Abstain from illegal sexual pleasures.
4. Abstain from falsehood.
5. Abstain from mind-clouding intoxicants.

Liberation of the soul, Buddha taught, is not to be achieved by the mere observance of prayer and sacred rites, but comes only as a final reward after a profound inner search for self. Man does not sin against God but against himself, hence the overwhelming importance to the Buddhist of proper thought and proper conduct. Depending on the life he has lived a man may be born again and again—sometimes to a higher state, sometimes as the lowest and most despised of creatures. From this stems the Buddhist conviction that all life, even to the flea on his robes or the weevil in his flour, is sacred. The flea may not be squashed. It may be someone's father or mother.

Tibetan Buddhism, called Lamaism, today embraces three million people within Tibet itself and almost as many more on the fringes of neighbouring Nepal, Bhutan and Sikkim, and is far removed from the original teachings of Gautama.

Within two centuries of his death, many of the followers of the Buddha began to modify the teachings of the master to fit them more to the everyday needs of the common man.

They sought a less demanding version of his creed with a greater importance on colourful ceremonial, and so the faith

C

became split into the two great sects of Buddhism today: The orthodox Hinayana, or "Little Vehicle", which largely adheres to the principle at least of Buddha's original teachings, and the Mahayana, or "Great Vehicle", which attaches great importance to endless prayer, dazzling ritual and in some countries embraces a whole series of lesser gods.

Lamaism in Tibet is a variant of Mahayana liberally tinged with the dark overtones of demonology stemming from the old primitive Tibetan religion of Bon Po. The Tibetan lives in a world swarming with gods and demons. He must propitiate the rolangs, the walking dead who stride blindly through the country, never moving aside and whose touch means death. There are the demons of the earth who forbid mining for gold and other treasures. There are the demons of the storm, demons of the mountains, demons of the rivers.

As they anticipated Darwin so did the simple Tibetans blindly grope centuries ahead of Pasteur in their belief that all diseases of the body are due to tiny invisible devils who lurk among filth and stench, flying out to attack the unwary human who passes too close.

Today religion suffuses Tibet. It is the essence of their everyday life, for prayer is everywhere. The great monasteries shelter thousands of monks who give their days and nights to prayer. Laymen murmur the sacred words, "*Om mani padme hum*"—"Hail to the jewel of the lotus"—hundreds of times a day. It is stamped on fragments of rice paper, flutters from flagstaffs in hill villages, is pinned to sacred cairns and revolves ceaselessly on the prayer wheels of every shrine and temple.

Religious merit is gained by the endless repetition of this phrase which to a Lamaist, who sees Buddha perpetually seated in a lotus flower, the symbol of rebirth, is spiritually equivalent to the Christian faith's Lord's Prayer.

Each time a prayer wheel revolves, the printed prayer goes winging away to the gods. Some of the prayer wheels or prayer barrels contain the "*Om Mani*" printed from wood blocks, over and over again, on the thinnest of rice paper and compressed into the barrel so that the prayer is multiplied in millions by each turn of the wheel.

Fear, amounting to terror of the demons, and dread of what an omission or shortcoming might condemn them to in their next reincarnation are the major driving forces behind the Tibetan's endless religious observances. The fly that drops in his buttered tea must be carefully lifted out and put to dry for it may be some poor soul paying penance for his shortcomings in his previous existence. And coming back as a fly, a flea, a pariah dog or some other lowly form of existence does not bring mental oblivion. The soul so un-cased, say the Tibetans, still has all the human ability to understand, to suffer and, presumably, to repent.

The ultimate ambition of a Lamaist is to pass out of human existence, having shed or overcome all earthly passions (there are 84,000 of these temptations, say the teachers) and enter the perfection of Nirvana.

But not all seek such escape. There are the Living Buddhas of the monasteries, several hundreds of them. These are monks who, having achieved enlightenment, are entitled to pass on but who, for the sake of the less fortunate, have renounced their release from earthly suffering to help other souls on their way. When a Living Buddha's body dies his soul passes into an infant, and the highest of the Living Buddhas are the Dalai and the Panchen Lamas, for they are the reincarnation of Tibet's two great guardian gods.

Just as Buddhism is split into differing sects so is Lamaism subdivided within itself. Dominating all in Tibet is the Gelukba or Yellow Sect whose monks wear the yellow hat. Of lesser influence are the Sakya, or Coloured Sect, the Ngingmapo (Red Sect) and the Kagupa (White Sect) all of whom wear red hats.

For more than a century after Basba, the Red Hat Lamas consolidated their power, and gradually Buddhism degenerated from the original teachings until it was hardly possible to tell it from the original devil worship. The stage was thus set for the arrival of another great figure in Tibet's history—Tsong Kaba the Reformer. He was a follower of the Gelukba Sect of the Yellow Hats—the name itself means roughly "Those taking the path to virtue". Tsong Kaba started reforming religion, casting out many of the devil-worshipping props and preaching a more austere life for the monks. On the temporal plane he was shrewd enough, too, to cultivate the friendship of the kings of Mongolia and the emperor of China, so that as decades passed the grand power of the Yellow Hats grew as one Grand Lama (not Dalai Lama) followed another.

By the time the fourth Grand Lama was in the ruling seat the Yellow Hats felt strong enough to challenge the rival Red Sect, and this was where the Yellow friendship with China bore fruit. With the help of the reigning emperor—a Mongolian Khan—the older and more degenerate Sakya religion was overthrown. The fifth Grand Lama, Ngawang Lobsang, was installed with full religious and temporal powers and was the first to assume the title of "Dalai" which is Mongolian for "Ocean wide wisdom".

The "Great Fifth", as he is often called, made many changes. He declared himself to be the reincarnation of the great guardian god of Tibet, Chenrezi, and so became the first of the long line of God-kings. He built the vast Potala palace in Lhasa, he enforced the Yellow Hats' rulings of celibacy and forbade the drinking of wine. And to ensure succession (not an easy matter for a celibate sect) he firmly established the doctrine that his soul on death would pass into the body of a child who would become the next Dalai Lama.

It was another of his divine revelations that unwittingly created a rivalry that has plagued Tibet to the present day. Wanting to honour his old tutor, the Dalai Lama decided that he (the tutor) was an incarnation of the guardian god Opami. Thus he, too, must be a Lama and the title of Panchen (Teacher) Lama was created for him.

The actual standing of the Dalai and Panchen Lamas has never clearly been defined, not even in Tibet, and there appears to be no hard and fast rules about it. Generally speaking the Dalai Lama has ruled supreme in matters both

spiritual and temporal in those parts of Tibet more sus-
ceptible to Indian influence, while the Panchen Lama has
always held greatest sway in the Chinese influenced areas.
As far as actual territory is concerned the Dalai Lama has
undoubtedly wielded more power and has been generally
accepted by the outside world as the head of the state. But
spiritually the Tibetans make little difference between them
and refer to them by the collective name of "Gyalwa Yapse"
which means "father and son" without saying which is
which.

As is so often the case the strong ruler was followed by a
weakling. The sixth Dalai Lama scorned the austerities of his
predecessor, and for him wine, feasting and women were
the spoils of office. He did not last long. His flight from
Lhasa led to strife among the rival sects and Tibet's neighbours were quick to seize the chance. First the Mongols and
then the Chinese overran the kingdom and for the next 300
years, broken only by sporadic and uncertain revolts, the
Manchu Dynasty of China maintained a kind of viceroy in
Lhasa, regarding Tibet as no more than a vassal state,
sometimes passive, sometimes turbulent and rebellious.

There were other incursions. The Ghurkas from Nepal
crossed the frontier more than once, to be thrown out either
by the Tibetans themselves or with the help of the Chinese
garrison that was maintained intermittently in the country.

This state of affairs continued until the beginning of the
twentieth century which saw penetration into Lhasa by a
British expeditionary force, the fall of the Manchu empire
and the rise of the Kuomingtang in China.

Britain first began to show an interest in Tibet soon after
the middle of the eighteenth century. Warren Hastings, first
Governor-General of India, established more or less friendly
contact with the then Regent of Tibet and tried to develop
some kind of trading relations, but they came to nothing.
Tibet was suspicious of the British, who were engaged in
taking over Bhutan and Sikkim which London regarded as
part of India, while Lhasa regarded them as outlying provinces of Tibet. Many attempts were made by Britain to

develop trade between the two countries but for more than a
century they failed completely. In 1890 Britain did sign a
Tibetan trade and frontier treaty with the Manchu over-
lords, but it was never enforced and in 1904, while the
Panchen Lama was flirting with the Czar of Russia, who
had ambitions in Asia, Britain launched its famous Young-
husband expedition.

The official task of Colonel (later Sir Francis) Young-
husband was to open up Tibet for trade. Probably the
hidden but major motive was to bar the way to further
Russian encroachments.

A relatively small British force under the command of
Brigadier-General J. L. MacDonald pushed over the
frontier from India and after a leisurely campaign of eight
months reached Lhasa in August 1904. But it was a poor
victory, for the thirteenth Dalai Lama had fled from the
Potala long before the British column arrived and negotiations could only be opened with a Regent. A treaty was
finally signed giving Britain the right to open trading centres
in three Tibetan towns and, as a sop to the tottering Manchu
empire, recognising China's suzerainty over Tibet. This
was followed by a further treaty between Britain and
Russia making Tibet a "buffer state" between them.

For four years the Dalai Lama wandered in exile in
China, finally starting back for Lhasa in 1909. His hopes of
an easy return were short-lived. Under the leadership of
General Chao-Erh-Teng, known as "the Butcher", a
Chinese army had crossed the border and was advancing on
Lhasa, burning monasteries and massacring monks on the
way. Once again the Dalai Lama fled, this time to British
India.

For three more years Tibet's ruler lived in exile waiting
for a turn of the wheel that might take him back to Lhasa.
It came in 1912, when the old Manchu régime of China
finally collapsed. The Lama returned and the centuries-old
play continued, the new China of the Kuomingtang claiming
over-lordship of Tibet and maintaining a "high com-
missioner" in Lhasa, the outside world holding a watching

brief, broken by occasional abortive conferences, and tacitly, if not openly, accepting that Tibet was little more than a satellite state of China.

The thirteenth Dalai Lama ruled long and, generally speaking, he ruled well. Remote from the world as he was, he was no novice at power politics, and strove continually to protect the interests of his country by playing off against each other the rival interests beyond his borders. Warned in 1933 by the state oracle that his end was approaching, he put the affairs of state in order and, murmuring, "I will take birth again," the sacred Living Buddha left his aged earthly body to seek a new one.

So we come to the Dalai Lama of the present day, the man whose story I am telling; and it might be pertinent, before outlining the manner of his discovery, to point out that I do not propose to enter into a discussion on the theory of reincarnation. I am concerned in this volume with the story of the Dalai Lama and the events leading to his escape. How he was discovered is to me utterly fascinating; but it does not follow that I believe him to be a reincarnated God-king. I cannot refrain, however, from commenting that, if the Dalai Lama is not the reincarnation of previous Lamas, and is not the Living God of Chenrezi, then in view of his wisdom, his tolerance, his political prescience and his saintliness, his life has been a fascinating experiment in the value of environment and early teaching, in which the wise elders of a country have seized a peasant boy and turned him into a great man.

There is of course no reason to disbelieve the way in which he was found. While the monks of the Potala chanted their liturgies on the death of the thirteenth Dalai Lama, the earthly corpse of their ruler was embalmed in yak butter and salt. Its features cased in gold leaf, the mummy was seated upright on the throne of the lesser audience hall of the Potala. For forty-nine days, the monks declared, the soul of their king would dwell by the waters of the sacred Lake Cho Khor Gye before leaving to take up residence in a newly-born infant, as yet unknown. Not till then did the seers and oracles begin their four-year search for the new body of the Living Buddha, the incarnation of Chenrezi, the Tibetan guardian "god of Mercy with the Penetrating Vision", the man I met at Tezpur.

The ruling Regent, in the absence of a Lama, made a pilgrimage to the sacred lake and looked into the prophetic waters of Cho Khor Gye where he saw in its depths a three-storeyed Lamasery with turquoise-studded roofs of gold and near by a twisting road that led to a peasant house with curious eaves and gables of a style that no one in Lhasa had seen before.

But where was it? The vision gave no clue. Search parties set out from Lhasa without success. Finally, the body of the thirteenth Lama, still sitting in mummified state on its Potala throne, is said, according to Tibetans, to have helped. His throne faced south. He was planted rigidly to face the same direction. But twice in one night, say the oracles, though the hall was locked to outsiders, the face of the dead ruler turned to the east. The oldest oracle in Tibet was consulted with this new information in mind.

"Look east," he told them. "Look beyond our border into China."

More expeditions set out and runners came back with the news that three children had been located, all of whom seemed possible candidates. The main expedition pushed on to the home of the first child, but it had died before they reached it. When they reached the second child it took one look at the monks and ran screaming in terror to its mother's skirts. The monks pushed on deep into the Chinese province of Tsinghai where thousands of Tibetans still live. There they approached the shores of Lake Koko-Nor, seeking the house of the third child, and there was the monastery, its three roofs gleaming gold and blue in the sunlight. There was the winding road, and there was the peasant home with the curious eaves and gables of the Regent's vision.

From the smoky kitchen, a small boy toddled towards the strange monks, laughing and unafraid, and as they watched him he began to shout: "Lama, Lama." His name they found, was Lhamo Dhondup, he was just over two years old but his eyes were bright and intelligent and he spoke with astonishing fluency for his years.

The monks were impressed but the child still had to go through the ritual tests. He passed the first ones with ease, giving the correct title of every dignitary in the party, even picking out some who had been purposely disguised as servants.

Sacred objects brought from Lhasa were spread out before him; rosaries, temple gongs, bells and ceremonial teacups. There were two of everything, identical to look at, but one set had been the personal property of the dead Dalai Lama. Unerringly the child picked out the true from the false.

He was shown two walking-staffs and for one moment the monks thought he had failed, for he picked up the wrong one. But before they could speak, he flung it away in disgust, took the right one and refused to be parted from it.

Only one final test remained. It was clear for all to see that the child had the outward physical characteristics—the large ears. He was gently stripped and the monks looked eagerly for the two moles which, tradition says, mark the places where the God's second pair of arms should be. The moles were there. Joyful runners set off ahead for Lhasa to announce that the new fourteenth Dalai Lama, the Lotus Thunderbolt, Great Precious Prince of the Soft Voice, Mighty in Speech, Excellent of Knowledge, Absolute in Wisdom, Holder of the Doctrine, the One Without Equal, Powerful Ruler of Three Worlds, the Ocean-Wise, had at last been found.

Hard as it had been to find the new God-king, it proved even harder to get him out of China, for the Chinese warlord of Tsinghai demanded £10,000 before he would let the boy leave. The Lamas paid and set out for Tibet. At the border they were stopped once again. The warlord wanted more money, and it took two years of negotiations and a further payment of £30,000 before the Dalai Lama, by then four years old, could go in triumph to the palace of Potala.

For little Lhamo it was the end of his childhood. In the

corridors of the 1,000-room Potala, he sat with his Lama tutors, learning the complex ceremonials and the Texts of Lamaism. Solemnly he endured the long hours of study without complaint. If he missed the joys of childhood he gave no sign and he learned quickly what was required of him.

In 1940, when he was five, the fourteenth Dalai Lama was lifted on to the seven-foot golden throne and gave his blessing to his family (his father was given a rank comparable to that of a duke) and to fur-hatted nobles and monks.

No one dared look up as the God-king was carried in procession round the five-mile sacred road, smooth with the tread of millions of pilgrims, which circles the city of Lhasa. Three million subjects gave devout thanks. Thousands of flickering butter-lamps lit Lhasa's night sky. This was the boy who was to flee the Chinese.

IV

THE "PEOPLE'S LIBERATION ARMY"

For ten peaceful years, while most of the outside world was torn by war or fear of war, the little God-king continued the studies that would fit him to be the heart of the faith of his three million subjects.

Hitler ravaged three-quarters of Europe and was smashed to final defeat while the Dalai Lama studied in his remote mountain fortress. Japan staked all on conquest and collapsed in ruin before the atom bomb. Chiang Kai-shek and Mao Tse-tung fought each other up and down the length of China, till Mao's Red Armies forced the old dictator to flee to his dream world of Formosa. The cold war succeeded the hot war. The Berlin airlift crisis had the outside world holding its breath as conflict once again seemed imminent.

But none of this touched the boy learning to be a ruler until 1949, when Mao Tse-Tung, following in the footsteps of the great Khans and the Manchu emperors, turned aside from hurling threats at Chiang Kai-shek and pondered on how best he could bring Tibet firmly into the orbit of his new China.

The blueprint for the twentieth-century conquest had already been laid out by power-mad dictators in the West a decade earlier, and so by 1949 Radio Peking had started the inevitable talk of Tibet's "enslaved people", of China's historic rôle, with Mao finally announcing that China must "liberate" the down-trodden people who were ignorant enough not even to know that they were down-trodden.

Lhasa listened and wondered, but that was all, as Mao mustered his "People's Liberation Army" on the frontiers. The Khamba tribesmen in the east cleaned their rifles and sent runners to Lhasa saying they were ready to fight the invader when the word was given. But Lhasa hesitated too long, and the two Regents, who were ruling the country during the God-king's religious education, were still consulting the oracles for guidance when Mao struck. In August 1950, from eight points along the frontier, his columns thrust into Tibet. The Khamba warriors, without word from Lhasa, melted away into the hills without a shot. There was no Tibetan army to bar the way. "Being a non-violent and peace-loving country Tibet had no stock of arms and ammunition," said the pathetic manifesto issued to the world from Lhasa.

As the "liberating forces" thrust deep into Tibet towards Lhasa the Regents and their counsellors turned to the United Nations and appealed for urgent intervention to check the aggressors. They received, instead, a piously worded expression of hope that the Tibetans and Chinese would arrange a compromise and live peacefully together. In fairness to the United Nations one must admit that it would have been hard for them to take any definite action and foreign intervention would have been quite impossible. Yet even if there was nothing the United Nations could do, a formal protest by India at that early stage may well have resulted in an immediate compromise. At first, as the Chinese columns reached Lhasa, the Tibetan leaders (so I was later told) were flabbergasted at the coolness with which Nehru received their cries of despair. They were not to know then that right through the Chinese–Tibet war, India would cynically ignore bonds of friendship with Tibet that had been forged centuries before, and bonds of religion too, because of her fear of the new China.

With no help forthcoming, the Regents in Lhasa turned again to the state oracle. What should their young God-king do? The oracle studied the portents, and advised the Dalai Lama to flee from the invaders.

Before he left Lhasa, the Dalai Lama was hurriedly invested with full power and the Regency was abolished. It was ironical that after the years of study he should finally become ruler of his country at a moment when it seemed to be on the point of disintegration.

A second and final appeal was sent from Lhasa to Lake Success, but there was no answer from the General Assembly. Nobody in the United Nations was very worried about the fate of a tiny, isolated nation that had no industry, no troops, no obvious wealth; nobody seemed to notice that by its very geographical location Tibet had a much greater importance, and might one day be a spring-board to the south for the new Chinese giant.

There was little fighting as the Chinese pushed on; little, that is, by modern standards of warfare. The small Tibetan frontier post at Chamdo put up a show of brief resistance but was swallowed effortlessly by the "liberators", as the Dalai Lama, his advisers and an escort of warrior tribesmen mounted on hill ponies left the Potala and headed south through the fog and snows over little-known tracks towards the Indian border.

Possibly the Dalai Lama had in mind some sanctuary in India and the formation of a government-in-exile, but he did not cross the frontier. The caravan halted in the Chumbi valley and the God-king opened long-range negotiations with Red China. The following May the Seventeen-Point Treaty was signed, under which Mao Tse-tung agreed to let Tibet retain a form of autonomous rule and promised that the powers and status of the Dalai Lama should remain unchanged. In return Tibet surrendered control of foreign affairs to Peking.

Today, eight years later, Tibet claims that the treaty, concluded under duress, was never valid, and insists that the Tibetan Governor had no power to offer the surrender of the Lhasa cabinet, adding that the terms were dictated arbitrarily to him in Chinese, he was made to translate them into Tibetan and then told to sign the agreement on behalf of the Dalai Lama on pain of more "liberation" armies being poured into the country. He protested that he had no authority and that in any case, by Tibetan custom, no treaty could be valid unless it was affixed with the official seal of the Kashak, duly authorised by the Dalai Lama. So a duplicate of the Kashak seal was made in China and, as far as Mao Tse-tung was concerned, everything was legal.

But though Tibet now repudiates the Seventeen-Point Treaty, at the time the country appeared to accept it and tried to adhere to its terms. When the Dalai Lama reached Tezpur in 1959, he said in his statement:

"In 1951, under pressure of the Chinese Government, a seventeen-point agreement was made between China and Tibet. In that agreement, the suzerainty of China was accepted as there was no alternative left to the Tibetans. But even in the agreement it was stated that Tibet would enjoy full autonomy. Though the control of External Affairs and Defence were to be in the hands of the Chinese Government, it was agreed that there would be no interference by the Chinese Government with the Tibetan religion and customs and her internal administration. In fact, after the occupation of Tibet by the Chinese armies, the Tibetan Government did not enjoy any measure of autonomy even in internal matters. . . . The Dalai Lama and his Government tried their best to adhere to the seventeen-point agreement, but the interference of the Chinese authorities persisted."

With a "treaty" signed, whether legally or not, Red China now faced the same problem that had baffled Khans, Manchus, and the Kuomintang alike over the preceding six centuries. How to maintain the land that had been won by their "liberation" armies? They turned to an old stratagem and attempted to wrest control of Tibet from the Dalai Lama by using his spiritual brother, the Panchen Lama, and to this end, even before the Seventeen-Point Treaty was signed, they announced the formation of a "Free Tibetan Government", headed by the Panchen Lama.

Both the Manchus and the Kuomintang had repeatedly tried to secure earlier Panchen Lamas as the leaders of a pro-Chinese opposition to the Dalai Lama, but had always failed, and when at last the previous Panchen Lama died in Chinese territory in 1937, the Chinese claimed to find his reincarnation in Sinkiang province. The Lhasa authorities, however, had refused to recognise the boy as a true reincarnation, or to admit him to Tibet unless he was accompanied by his Chinese guard, but now the Communists decided to use the same thirteen-year-old boy, apparently gambling that Tibetans would be unwilling to take up arms against one of the two supreme "Living Buddhas" in spite of the dispute over his authenticity.

The young Dalai Lama now faced a new problem. Not all Tibetans were prepared to condemn the Chinese out of hand at this stage, and there were sections of the people who argued that even remote Tibet could not sit in her ancient mists, "by the world forgot", and who urged a break with the feudal past and clamoured for their backward country to learn something of modern methods. Their argument was that the Chinese were there in Tibet, it was a *fait accompli*, so why not learn from them?

So the Dalai Lama returned to Lhasa to receive the first Red emissaries, who spread out an enticing programme before him, by which schools, roads, hospitals would be built, light industries would be established, some of Tibet's mineral resources would be tapped.

To much of this the Lama agreed, for he could hardly do anything else, but the rosy programme started to go wrong almost from the start. Slowly at first, but with the tempo increasing rapidly as their grip tightened, the Chinese started diminishing Tibetan authority; the rights and powers of Tibetan officials from the top down to the smallest district officer were whittled away. The officials were forced to pledge support for the Chinese occupation army and to join in "expelling imperialist influences". Forced labour was called on for a vast road-building programme and great highways and airfields were constructed, absorbing large tracts of the country's scarce agricultural land. Shrines were demolished and villages cut in two.

The mass of Tibetans did not outwardly object for the very good reason that they had not the means of doing so, but subsequent events have shown beyond any doubt how bitterly these "reforms" were resented. In a land where one third of the men are monks, where religion is the dominating force of everyday life, it was not surprising, as one observer put it, that they should feel "the inner perfection of a man's soul was of more importance than asphalt on a road", and as the Dalai Lama is reported to have said more than once: "China and Tibet are like fire and wood."

The advent of many thousands of Chinese soldiers and civilian technicians brought a further problem: how were they to be fed? Not from Peking, obviously. So, as is the age-old way of conquering armies, whatever their political creed, they lived "off the land". Tibet is a thinly populated country for its size and its produce was normally no more than sufficient, with a little left over for emergencies, to feed its own people. Essential food supplies soon became short, prices rose and before long the Chinese angered the Tibetans still further by raiding the ancient granaries where the food reserves were kept. When that was exhausted they laid hands on the country's reserves of gold and silver bullion, explaining this away as "loans" to buy further food and to help in the work of bringing Marxist enlightenment to Tibet. From this it was only a step to printing Chinese paper currency, declared to be the legal tender, but to this day stoutly rejected by the common people.

In 1954 the Dalai Lama, now eighteen and imbued with a boy's natural curiosity in spite of (or perhaps because of) his years of seclusion, made the journey to Peking to see for himself what Mao Tse-tung's particular brand of Communism had done for China. Some say he had no choice anyway, and that he was taken there rather than invited.

The last drop of publicity and propaganda was squeezed out of the trip by the Chinese, who made great play of speeches in which he was declared to have praised Mao and all his works. He was seen in public, apparently on the best of terms with the Panchen Lama, and Tibet was flooded with hastily printed photographs of the two "Living Gods" deep in fraternal conversation over bowls of tea. Everything in fact was done to show how happy and friendly everybody

The Prologue of *The Charitable Prince* being performed in
Kalimpong as part of the Losar (New Year) celebrations

The abbot of a monastery at Gyangtse telling his beads
outside the monastery door

The road to Tibet: Ralph Izzard and the author catch this shot of their coolies crossing a primitive bridge high over a mountain river was, and how the Chinese "big brother" was devoted to building a new and happier way of life for his poor backward brethren in Tibet.

There was only one thing wrong with this: nobody believed it, least of all the Tibetans who stayed at home.

V

APPEAL FOR HELP

The conquest of Tibet seemed complete, and with Chinese colonisers in their millions crawling across its landscape, Tibet had become just another name in the long list of countries subjugated by the "liberation forces" of Communism. It was certainly the last country in the world where one would expect any revolt to be staged.

Very little news of Chinese activities in the country, or the disquieting potential problems they posed for the West, reached the free world. With a ruthlessness only to be expected, China curtained Tibet off from any contact which might have aroused sympathy for the conquered or hostility to the conquerors. A few vague mutterings of discontent, a few vague rumours of sporadic fighting by the Tibetans reached India, only to be hastily repressed in the cause of Sino–Indian solidarity.

There is no doubt that from 1952 onwards Indian Government officials were receiving regular and disturbing reports of unrest in Tibet from their office in Lhasa and even more ominous news of Chinese troop movements near the borders of India's northern states, and it is one of the sorriest aspects of Tibet's struggle that Nehru decided that any news about Tibetan resistance should be quietly pigeon-holed, and for several years pursued a deliberate policy of hiding any unpalatable (i.e., anti-Chinese) truths from members of the British Commonwealth who might have been more concerned with the spread of Communism than he was.

Unfortunately for him, there was a serious uprising in Tibet in 1956, news of which could not be kept secret, perhaps partly because restive politicians in India, whose sense of conscience was a little sharper than their leader's, saw to it that details of the revolt were disseminated to responsible people outside the Government; and so for the first time the Western world began to realise that though Tibet was by now to all intents a province of China, there were some people in it who were still determined to fight. It also made sympathisers with Tibet, and many Tibetans themselves were acutely aware that Nehru's conduct in the affair did not perhaps conform to standards high enough for them to repose any future trust in his public utterances.

The serious nature of the revolt was emphasised in a letter to the *Calcutta Statesman* shortly afterwards when Thupten Nyenjeh, abbot of Gyangtse monastery and governor of Gyangtse province, wrote that he had recently left Lhasa and felt that the gravity of the situation in Tibet was not fully known.

"A full-scale war of independence is now raging in eastern and north-eastern Tibet and the people of the provinces of Lithang, Bha, Chantin, Menyak, Nyarong, Horkhok, Mheli, Rongpatsa, Dzachukha, Sertha, Dhema, Derge and Nanchen have driven out all Chinese troops after savage fighting," he stated.

"Only the heavily fortified air base of Kardzeh holds out against the Tibetans, who now control an area of approximately 210 square miles. This grows larger as the fighting spreads steadily towards Lhasa.

"It has always been the desire of Tibet to live in peace and amity with fellow nations, which makes all the more distressing her need to fight for traditional freedom."

The uprising of 1956 certainly had one immediate benefit for the Tibetan cause, for though in itself an heroic failure, it made people in the free world realise that if guerrillas could stage one such revolt, there might have been others before and there could be more in the future.

The 1956 revolt, as it is now called, was the work of an underground movement, carefully organised and reasonably well armed, which planned a mass attack on the Chinese at more than a hundred points on April 16, 1956. It could never have been a total success, but it might have achieved limited successes had not the Lamas of Litang monastery, due south of Lhasa and about a hundred miles from the Bhutan border, become impatient and launched an attack at the end of March before the general plan was completed. In a fierce battle 600 Tibetans from the monastery led peasants in an attack against a Chinese cavalry unit. Only seven Tibetans were alive when the battle was over. Within a few days the monastery was surrounded and under heavy fire from machine-guns.

For four days Litang monastery held out, but on April 3 the Chinese brought in heavy aircraft and started bombing it. Two days later resistance at Litang ended. Yet, though the world did not know this at the time, the real nation-wide fighting against the Chinese can be said to have started from this date. The news that the Chinese had bombed a holy monastery spread slowly across the country, and word went round that the rebellion had started.

The first to break into open active opposition to the Chinese over-lords were the warlike nomads of the border province of Kham. The Khambas, who are more powerfully built than the average Tibetan, had already seen their cattle driven off the grazing lands they had used for centuries and taken to collective settlements. Now the monasteries were being looted and their lands seized. So the Khambas, who are to Tibet what the Pathans and Afridis are to India, hit back. Chinese convoys were ambushed at surprise road-blocks in the winding trails from the border. Military posts were attacked by night. Snipers lurked behind the rocks and picked off any Chinese soldiers who came into range.

Among their leaders was a giant of a man, his bullet-head shaven and who adopted as his fighting name General Tobgye Wangdue, "The Powerful Subduer". It was going to take two years; but two years later, at a lonely pass on the Tibetan frontier, Tobgye Wangdue and I met, and it was from him and his followers, at a small camp high in the Himalayas, that I was able to find out for the first time the full scale of the Tibetan fighting and how it was organised.

The Chinese retaliated vigorously to the guerrilla attacks.

Garrisons were strengthened, planes flew low over the passes, more monasteries were bombed. Suspect Khambas were rounded up in hundreds, religious teachers were arrested and ordered to teach the Marxist creed. Those who refused just "vanished". Inconclusive guerrilla warfare raged up and down the Kham province as Peking introduced more and more repressive measures. Religion was now openly declared to be the enemy. Soldiers used holy images of the Buddha for target practice, books and scriptures were burned, more and more Lamas were seized and executed, and as word of these excesses spread, so did the fires of revolt creep nearer to Lhasa. Displaced Khambas moved from their home grounds and roused the tribesmen as far west as the Tsangpo valley. There were few waverers. Mao Tse-Tung's men, far from crushing their semi-primitive neighbours, had started something they could not control, a spirit of nationalism, probably the strongest upsurge since the golden days of Songtsen Gompo.

All this was virtually unknown to the free world (excepting India). The 1956 revolt received a brief mention in the world's press, but such reports as appeared were necessarily short and often unconfirmed, and within a few days Tibet ceased to appear as a newspaper headline. So far as the world was concerned, it was a coup that had failed—as it was in fact bound to fail—and there was no suggestion that it had started off a chain reaction which would eventually lead to the revolt at Lhasa and the flight of the Dalai Lama.

For two years there was little news of Tibet, though now we know that for long periods the Khamba guerrillas were operating in force against the Chinese. But in July 1958 I received a long letter translated from the Tibetan and which arrived at my Paris flat through a curious chain of circumstances. It was addressed from Kalimpong in West Bengal, signed by a Tibetan acquaintance I had previously met in Kalimpong, and who was now obviously one of the leaders of a group of Tibetans in India anxious to attract world attention to the plight of their country. The letter, which was dated July 14, 1958, read:

"Dear Mr. Barber,

"It is many months since we last drank tea together but I have the most earnest memories of your interest in Tibet and your displeasure with Communism, and in a few days from this date a group of prominent Tibetans in Kalimpong will be sending out a manifesto to many countries of the world. Because of our old acquaintanceship I must tell you some of the news of our beloved country which we trust the free countries of the world will publish.

"You must know that since 1950 when the Chinese Communists invaded our land with about five hundred thousand of their so-called 'liberation army' they settled some four million Chinese immigrants in the eastern and north-eastern regions. These settlers, along with their powerful armies, have attempted to destroy our religion, culture and traditions. There has been merciless treatment of our people by the Chinese, and many have had to flee to the far-off deserts and valleys, so that now our people are fighting for freedom, and hundreds are being killed daily by the Chinese in fierce battles.

"There is trouble in Lhasa, the capital of Tibet. Recently some thirty thousand people from the southern areas had to leave their property, families and settled life to save themselves from the brutal treatment of the Chinese over-lords. Now without homes, these people are also out in the deserts and it is feared that there may be uprisings in the south and central areas, as a consequence.

"Not only have the Chinese Communists occupied our country, making every effort to exploit our people, but they have also made Tibet into a huge arsenal that can have no other conceivable purpose than a future offensive against her neighbouring countries and the world at large. They are building army barracks, forts, bridges and airfields at strategic places, and their extensive programme for constructing great roads and railways is mainly to accelerate the movement of their armed forces.

"Pray help us if you can. We stand for religion and though yours is not the same as ours, you too would not like

to see your monasteries bombed and your priests murdered.
My blessings to you."

This letter, I afterwards discovered, contained sections of a
longer letter and manifesto which was soon afterwards sent
to the United Nations. My reaction to it was twofold. I
knew well my friend (who is best un-named, because he
figures again shortly in a most important rôle) as an honour-
able man who would never have lent his name or authority
to any letter in which he did not believe. In other words, he
was telling the truth about conditions in Tibet, and therefore
the letter was of the utmost importance. Secondly, since I
knew him, and had indeed many other excellent friends in
Kalimpong and Darjeeling, it might be well worth my while
making the journey to Kalimpong, not so much to gather
extra information (which could be nothing more than
rumour) but to sound out the possibility of making some
contact with the Tibetan fighters themselves.

There were many ways in which this might be done.
Though the Indians have barred Sikkim to Britishers unless
they acquire special passes (always for some reason very
tardily granted!) why could I not be smuggled across the
mountains to the border? If this were not feasible, it might
be possible to reach one of the several high passes along the
Tibet-Nepal border, and across which Tibetans in the guise
of monks or traders pass regularly. On the other hand there
was no point in getting to the frontier of Tibet (even suppos-
ing it were possible) in the vague hope of picking up a snippet
or two of news from some passing wayfarer. It had to be all
or nothing. I myself was passionately interested in dis-
covering what was happening, and it so happened that Mr.
Arthur Wareham, the editor of my newspaper, the *Daily
Mail*, shared with me not only a natural interest in events
clothed in secrecy but (above and apart from our duties as
journalists) a real deep and genuine feeling that we should
be doing a service to the world in general if we were able to
expose the wicked machinations of a régime seeking to
impose its will by force on a country that had no territorial

ambitions, and whose foreign policy consisted entirely of requesting foreigners to leave them in peace to continue their solemn devotions and their peaceful non-belligerent lives.

It so happened that Arthur Wareham visited Paris shortly afterwards and we dined together and talked the matter over at some length. Again and again he emphasised what both of us felt so strongly and which had nothing to do with our professional viewpoints: the utter wickedness of fighting this one country above all others, one of the most spiritual countries in the world, a land which asked for neither friend nor foe, and which did not even constitute a buffer (and so permit some sort of pseudo-military excuse) against her only neighbour, a timid India which would no more dare to fight China than she would the United States.

That evening I drove Arthur back to the Ritz and later wrote a careful letter to Kalimpong. I did not send it direct, as the Indians had not only searched my bags on my previous visit to Kalimpong, but had tampered with my mail. I despatched it to Calcutta, with an arrangement for it to be taken to Kalimpong by hand at a suitable time by one of the many people travelling up there regularly.

The reply took some time to reach me, and it read:

"Dear friend Mr. Barber,
"Your heart is good and we need all friends. Rely on me for help if it is possible but do not count on being able to enter Sikkim and reach the border. However, many great Tibetan warriors are fighting along Nepal's northern frontier and we have contact with them from time to time. Come here first and see us, tread quietly, and be prepared for two months of hardship in Nepal if you wish to travel to see our friends whom I will arrange for you to meet. I hope you are in good health for the road is hard and long, as it always is to the truth."

I was in very good health, and I was very, very excited. I flew to London the next morning for a round-table conference. It would be a costly journey for it would require financing an expedition with porters, Sherpas, and equipment that would have to be flown from Britain. I would have to supply myself with sufficient food to last a minimum of two months. But I found myself engulfed in enthusiasm.

Only one thing worried me. Nepal, if Nepal it were to be, would not be a dangerous expedition, though to me, with a horror of heights, it would be a frightening one. But it was strange territory to me, and to be frank, I did not relish the idea, in my forty-ninth year, of walking three or four hundred miles across the Himalayas without at least one white companion. It was not that I did not trust the Sherpas, but I would probably be more than two weeks' journey from the nearest white man (particularly the nearest doctor), I spoke very little Hindustani, and though I knew I was fit enough to make the trip I felt that if by any chance I were injured, the presence of a fellow Britisher would at least give me moral support.

In my mind I knew immediately the perfect man to accompany me—Ralph Izzard, one of my colleagues, and famous the world over as the man who just walked 18,000 feet up Everest to find out how Hillary and Hunt were progressing during their conquest of the earth's highest mountain. Izzard knew the terrain, he had been the key member of a remarkable six-month expedition to hunt for the Abominable Snowman or yeti. He was absolutely fearless, and his lanky frame (he is six feet four inches) hid a quiet gentle individual with whom it would be quite impossible to pick a quarrel.

On the other hand I felt that any despatches about Tibet, incorporating, as they would, highly individual impressions, emotions and points of view, were best written by one man only, and as such it was probably far too much to ask Izzard to accompany me in a rôle which, however important, would inevitably be minor to mine, not in judgments and decisions, but in the actual business of gaining information and then writing it.

"But you're quite right," said Arthur Wareham. "Ralph is the perfect man; if you can persuade him, then I'm certainly agreeable to his going with you."

Fortunately for me, Ralph needed no persuasion. He was absolutely delighted, and accepted within five seconds of my first tentative approach. And so it was decided. Ralph, with his expert knowledge, would be in complete charge of all the physical arrangements necessary for the journey. I hoped that I would, after visiting Kalimpong, be able to say to Izzard, "I want to be at such and such a point on such a day," and he would get me there. The arrangements worked admirably. With his expert experience to guide him, Ralph chose our tents, high-altitude equipment, and other gear which we had to buy in London. He arranged with the Westminster Hospital for all our injections to be of double strength. He supervised the purchase of drugs and medicines that we were to use not only for our own party, but for wounded Tibetans.

He was a tower of strength. In fact I do not hesitate to say that if Ralph had not been with me, I could not have succeeded in my mission. He "nursed" me over the high passes when my heart quailed with fear, he knew every camping spot, he knew where the best water was in the remotest regions, and he guided me to my rendezvous so that I reached it exactly on time. I could never have got there on my own.

By mid-September, 1958, little more than two months after I had received the letter from Kalimpong, there was serious news of heavy fighting in Tibet, and it was spreading westwards every day. *The Daily Telegraph*, particularly, printed some excellent detailed accounts of what was happening from George Patterson in Darjeeling. It looked as though my friend in Kalimpong had not been overstating the case and I felt more than ever the urge to be on the march. Fortunately by this time our preparations were well advanced.

Our first problem had been to get permission to enter Nepal without arousing any suspicions that our reason for visiting the land of the Gurkhas was to make contact with the Tibetans. This we did by applying for permission to enter as a small scientific expedition. Ralph is a Fellow of the

Zoological Society and this lent a certain credence to our pleas. (In fact it was very odd, both in London and later in Katmandu, the real reason for our excursion never for a moment entered the heads of the authorities. They were all convinced that our "scientific expedition" to catch voles and search for orchids was an elaborate excuse for a final attempt to find the Abominable Snowman. We were both delighted that they should think us so naïve.)

We had a hundred and one things to do during the two weeks it took for our visas to be granted. A large sum of money was transferred to a bank in Katmandu, Ralph took me to buy everything from double sleeping-bags to whistles in case we lost each other. Ralph decided to do the long walk in a pair of practice hockey boots, while I relied on my old Clark's desert boots, which lasted me throughout the trip. But we had also to be measured for heavy mountain boots, windproof clothes and so on. On Ralph's advice we decided not to use the ordinary waffle-weave long under-pants, but chose instead flannel pyjama trousers, which, when used as underclothes, give more freedom of movement during tough climbing.

One of the most astonishing things about the expedition was the way the preparations all clicked into position in a matter of days. Normally men prepare for weeks if not months for such an undertaking in such wild and desolate country. We had everything fixed in three weeks—even to my most personal request, which was for a large quantity of sulphur drugs for dysentery. (I had gone down with an appalling dose of dysentery in Jordan during the summer, and I did not fancy a recurrence on mountain trails. West-minster came up nobly with a thousand tablets guaranteed to knock out even bacillary dysentery in five days.)

Though Ralph was rightly quite capable of ordering every-thing we needed, from pins to ice-picks, I strongly urged two small items of luxury—folding arm-chairs. Weighing little more than two pounds each, we bought them at Benjamin Edgington's; they were the best value of anything we bought, and for a month we could see them strapped across porters' backs in the distance, the aluminium legs shining in the sun, and each sundown they were always ready, opened up, with tea and the rum bottle on an upturned packing-case, when we camped for the night.

On Sunday, November 16, we left London, our first destination being Calcutta, with a bill for overweight of nearly £300. From Calcutta we decided to split forces for a few days. Ralph would go to Darjeeling to pick the Sherpas from his old friends of previous expeditions; I would proceed to Kalimpong to see my friends and make plans.

We left all our heavy equipment at Dum-Dum, Calcutta's airport, and took the plane together to Bagdogra, the nearest place to either Darjeeling or Kalimpong where air-craft can land. From there one must do the last fifty miles by taxi. I little thought when I stepped out at Bagdogra, which is also the airport for Siliguri where the Dalai Lama halted, that within a few months I should be back again, rushing to Kalimpong and then across country to Siliguri and on to Tezpur to meet the God-king.

Ralph went off to Darjeeling and I took an ancient taxi, with a fiercely-driving chauffeur, and tore up the winding, treacherous road to Kalimpong until, with a sigh of relief three hours later, I dumped my bags in the dark hall of the one and only Himalayan Hotel, run by the three daughters of David MacDonald, who spent over twenty years in Tibet. They are three wonderful women and I have known them for many years and they seemed as delighted to see me as I was to see them.

The Himalayan Hotel has large rooms, with adjoining cubicles to which boys bring hot water for the tin tubs; the gardens riot with flowers, everything from magnolia to poinsettia. You can see six countries from the front door, and on fine days you can see both the snows of Kangchen-junga 27,000 feet in the skies, and the tropical river Teesta nearly 5,000 feet below. I love Kalimpong very much; it is one of my favourite places, alive with rumour, equally alive with Tibetans, for it is one of the few holes in the iron curtain and the end of the journey for the Tibetan muleteers bringing wool and hides from Lhasa to sell in India.

I stayed nearly a week in Kalimpong and it seemed clear, to say the least of it, that the Chinese occupation troops were finding it extremely difficult to put down guerrilla attacks against their garrisons and their lines of communication. The raids which first started in 1956 when the Khambas rose up in arms against the Chinese were by now assuming dangerous and unmanageable proportions for Red China.

The first official Chinese acceptance of "troubled conditions" had come on July 21, 1958, at a public meeting in Lhasa at which a written statement by the Dalai and Panchen Lamas was read out. Their official statement was shown to me in Kalimpong and it said: "The Dalai Lama calls on all Tibetans to be alert and guard against subversive plots in Tibet by imperialist elements, secret agents of Chiang Kai-shek and a handful of reactionaries inside Tibet."

Not only was this the first public admission made by the Chinese (for the Chinese drafted the Dalai Lama's public speeches and statements) about the presence of "subversive plots" but it was also the first time the Chinese accused Chiang Kai-shek's agents of activities inside Tibet. It was an interesting point, though there was no proof of help from the Chinese in Formosa and it might easily have been a deliberate "plant" by Peking. It was a useful line for them to take, anyway.

As usual the fighting in Tibet was increasing because of reprisals on both sides, but one must not forget that apart from Tibetan wrath at the burning of their monasteries, even the humblest Tibetans were deeply offended by the political pressures being exerted on them by the Chinese, pressures which took no account of historical facts. Later (in March 1959, as the Dalai Lama was escaping) George Patterson, who was with me at Tezpur, summed up these political stresses admirably in an article in *The Daily Telegraph* when he wrote in part:

"The Tibetans aver that at all conferences to determine the status of Tibet the Chinese have made no attempt to appeal to history or to produce any documents to support their claims. They have not even referred to Tibet's temporary association with the Manchu emperors, but base all their claims on Gen Chao's armed conquest of 1904-11, refusing to recognise that their claim is negated by later Tibetan action.

"The Tibetans feel they have been made a pawn of in the game of power politics. They maintain that it has only been the shifts of policies among the major Powers—Britain, China, Russia, India—at different periods which have made Tibet first an autonomous State under the suzerainty of China (Anglo–Chinese Treaty of 1890), then a buffer State (Anglo–Russian Treaty of 1907), and latterly a Chinese province (Sino–Indian Treaty of 1954).

"It is this last treaty (the origin of the famous 'five principles of peaceful coexistence') that is relevant to the present situation. The Tibetans declare that it is invalid because no Tibetan was represented.

"The Tibetans protested to the United Nations against Chinese aggression in 1950 and again in 1958, and had appealed to India for help time again. They have been frustrated and repulsed and discouraged from appealing to other nations because help would have to come through India, and this India would not allow."

George Patterson is a remarkable man who has spent much time in Tibet, and I had long talks with him in Kalimpong, but, on the whole, I think the less said about my week in Kalimpong the better. The police were round very quickly, but this time I had no evidence that they searched my bags, perhaps because I had bought a new briefcase with a combination lock. I had need for some place to store papers which were extremely private, for some of my time in Kalimpong was spent in tracing maps of the frontier region which included the latest dispositions of Chinese troops, guerrilla headquarters, and progress of the Chinese colonisers. The absence of maps of Tibet has always been a nuisance, but in a few days I had a set of rough maps which gave me all the details I required.

But naturally most of my time was spent making arrangements for the future. After three or four days of long discussions, and innumerable cups of tea, in which I was passed from man to man in many different areas in and around Kalimpong, I was left in no doubt that the Tibetans in the district knew exactly what was happening in their country. It was finally arranged that I should travel to the Solar Khumbu area of Nepal, an arduous but not dangerous journey, turn northwards at a given point, and there I would make contact with the guerrilla chief known as Tobgye Wangdue. The arrangements were invested with some theatrical trappings, partly because of the Tibetans' love of drama, partly because it was highly necessary. Wangdue was operating north of Nepal, and I was assured that he would keep any rendezvous made with me. But he would first send an emissary, whose name—or password, if one prefers—was to be Dondub, "Achievement of aim". Dondub would wait at a specified point for me for ten days— between December 14 and 24. When I arrived he would fetch Wangdue.

It was as simple as that—providing I could walk 200 miles at over 10,000 feet fairly quickly, for the only danger by now was the time element. When I left Kalimpong it was November 28. I landed in Calcutta and met Ralph, who, after engaging the Sherpas, had returned to Calcutta to buy food supplies, and that night we rang up Indian Airlines to book two seats for Katmandu, the capital of Nepal and starting-point of the trek to the border. To our consternation we found there was no free seat on any aircraft for ten days. The next morning we started the ancient pastime of string-pulling, and after several hours of violent argument were promised one seat in three days, another in four days. This was cutting things a bit fine, for there would surely be some delay in Katmandu, but then we ran into a real problem. Even with our two seats, the airline flatly refused to off-load any more passengers for our excess baggage, which by now, with all the food, amounted to over half a ton.

There was only one thing to be done and it had to be done

quickly. I had no time to discuss the matter with my office, so I chartered a twenty-six seater Dakota to fly the two of us and our baggage up the next morning. It cost about £300 for the two-hour flight, but there was no alternative. On Sunday, November 30, we landed at Katmandu airport, ready for five gruelling days of preliminary bribing and red tape before we could finally set off.

I had never visited Nepal before and almost from the moment we arrived we were hedged in by problems, most of which were solved by the discreet payment of money. When our eleven cases of food were being unloaded a Customs officer told us flatly that in no circumstances could he permit us to import our fifty tins of corned beef as it was banned from the country on religious grounds. It cost a bribe of thirty rupees to solve that problem, which the Customs officer did most neatly by merely crossing out the word "beef" on our manifest and substituting the word "mutton". We had two large square boxes labelled "Photographic development fluid—fragile", and this he viewed with suspicion, but on giving a written promise to export any of the fluid which remained unused, this was allowed to pass through. It was fortunate for us that it was not examined as each large carton contained a case of Scotch whisky, also banned from Katmandu on religious grounds.

In the government offices, our mission was highly suspect, but as the suspicion was always that we were going to attempt to find the yeti we rather encouraged it.

It should be explained that the Nepalese charge large fees for various expeditions, the largest of all being for yeti hunters, and also that they limit the number of expeditions; people stake their claim in Nepal for an attempt on Everest, or an expedition in search of yeti or blue poppies, and others are then not welcome if in pursuit of the same objects, and we had to undergo long cross-examinations at the foreign office. However, Mr. Singh, deputy secretary of the foreign ministry, obviously very worried about yeti possibilities, finally thought he had nailed me down by writing me as follows:

The author's camp in the courtyard of a Buddhist monastery

A Tibetan emissary

"Dear Mr. Noel Barber,

"I write this to confirm the permit granted by His Majesty's Government for yourself and Mr. Ralph Izzard to visit and stay in Solar Khumbu area for two months with effect from December 4, 1958, to February 3, 1959.

"As we have separate rules and regulations for mountaineering and Yeti Expeditions, you are advised not to indulge in any activity whatsoever during your stay in Solar Khumbu directly or indirectly directed to collect information regarding the existence of yeti or taking photographs relating thereon. Kindly send a reply to confirm that you will be abiding by the advice given above."

After a suitable hesitation, suspiciously noted, I wrote Mr. Singh a letter regretfully accepting these conditions. Ralph collected the last of our forty coolies together, changed £500 into one-rupee notes to pay the porters their various advances, and our four Sherpas arrived by train from Darjeeling. The next day, after an excellent dinner of roast peacock, we set off for the mountains.

E

VI

MEETING WITH A RESISTANCE LEADER

It took us sixteen days to reach our rendezvous with General Tobgye Wangdue on the Tibetan frontier, and to me the walk across the Himalayas was a fascinating experience, as different from the South Pole, where I had spent the previous winter, as Africa is from India. I had never climbed anything larger than the Yorkshire dales before I was jerked into this vertical existence of peaks and passes, of staircases of boulders many miles long and leading to the next camp thousands of feet above or below, and where we could camp each night, with our tents by the camp-fire in our own star-studded world, wrapped in a silence so profound that we hardly dared to break it with speech.

Those evenings as we struggled upwards to the high passes to find out at last what was happening in Tibet were among the most wonderful I have ever spent. Time after time, waiting for our supper, listening to the low crooning prayers of our Sherpa porters, I would wonder what on earth I was doing there, force-marching across some of the world's most arduous country and completely cut off from the rest of the world. Even during the previous winter, when I spent so many weeks at the South Pole, I had not been so isolated from the rest of humanity as on this march. It did not matter what happened, the rest of the world could blow itself up, it would probably be at least a fortnight before we received news of it. It was a wonderful feeling, as we plodded on, twice climbing to 14,000-foot passes, with the greatest scenery in the world encircling us like a giant panoramic postcard.

Ralph Izzard had made the physical arrangements admirably. In addition to our forty coolies, we had four

Sherpas, whom he had engaged at Darjeeling, each of them speaking Tibetan and Nepali as well as a smattering of English. Three of them had already worked with Ralph and knew every inch of the country leading eastwards from Katmandu. For our sirdar we had Ang Tsering, a grizzled old warrior of the Himalayas, now nearly fifty, but as tough as a man half his age. Ang Tsering's real duties were to keep everybody else in order, and particularly to watch over those coolies carrying important supplies—one man for instance carried nothing but the money; another a case of whisky, each coolie carrying up to 60 lb.

Our cook was Pemba, more likable as a man than as a cook. For the most part Pemba, who had sorrowful watery eyes like a dog's, dressed in a pair of blue linen trousers which he rolled up when we arrived at camp, showing long greyish underwear. He had an old colonel's hacking-jacket, baksheesh from some long forgotten trek, and he was an indefatigable walker. He would be the last to leave when we struck camp each morning, then would pass us on the way, and arrive at the next night's camp long before us, so that when we arrived there would be a mug of tea waiting, the rum on an upturned box, and the tents ready with hurricane lamps so that we could slide into our sleeping-bags for a read before supper.

In addition we each had a personal servant. All this sounds very luxurious, but in fact it is so much a custom in the Himalayas that I do not think one could travel without a personal Sherpa. Mine was a tough giant of a man called Adjeeba, a "tiger", and I wrote in my diary one night, as I watched him at work, "Dark hair, never seems to need a real shave. Strong hands, tiny thumb nails. Wears a peaked hat with flaps tied on top and an ancient parka over grey woollen pullover. Very small feet. Trousers rather like G.I. fatigue denims tucked into stockings during the march. Also has a handsome pair of knickerbockers, stripped under knees, which he wears with very short nylon socks and a strip of brown leg in the middle as in France. He can carry two full rucksacks as easily as one. Washes my shirts each night then dries them by fastening them to rucksack during march—portable clothes line."

Ralph took Adjeeba's son, who was being brought up in the Sherpa tradition by his very strict father. He was a fine boy of about eighteen.

On these four men depended at least the comforts of our expedition and the discipline among the porters, who were half Nepalese, half Tibetan or Namche Bazar Sherpas, a gay, colourful lot, but given to drinking *chung*, the local beer (with the colour and consistency of porridge), whenever they could find some at any of the tiny settlements we passed from time to time.

Each day started at 6 a.m. when a softly crooning voice approached my tent. The voice belonged to Pemba, the cook, bringing in "bed tea", always with a murmuring, wordless song. I asked him what he was singing.

"Nothing, sahib," he replied, "I only sing a little so you won't be wakened too suddenly." The tent flap open, Pemba wriggled forward on his stomach so that his wet boots would not dirty my groundsheet, and set the mug of hot sweet tea on still another wooden food packing-case which Adjeeba put in the tent each night as a table for my lamp and books. "Bed tea" was followed by a wash in hot water, and then breakfast of porridge or tinned bacon and eggs, with toast or biscuits and marmalade. Pemba had orthodox ideas about cooking. For instance, he could not possibly understand that scrambled eggs could *ever* be served except on toast. Toast was not merely something rather pleasant to eat with scrambled eggs, it was actually part of the double word "scrambled eggs". Pemba was thus thrown into a state of the utmost confusion when, all our bread having been eaten, I casually said I would prefer my eggs scrambled instead of fried for breakfast. There being no bread, he resourcefully produced a breakfast which included scrambled eggs on chocolate biscuits.

What I did not realise until I was on the trail was that the distances one travels daily are all prearranged, for the simple reason that though we (and the four Sherpas) had tents, nobody else did. In fact many of the coolies (who were paid 3s. 6d. a day) preferred to carry even their shoes and climb barefoot. This meant that they had to have some shelter at nights, especially at height, and so we moved forward daily in a series of stages, anything up to fifteen miles a day, always camping within a mile or so of some settlement or farm which had sheds in which the coolies could sleep. Pemba chose our own particular camps, always with an eye to good water supplies, and after advice from Ralph, and never too far from the porters' shelters.

The food we carried in wooden boxes which Ralph had had crated in Calcutta. Each was nailed down, and after we had decided on the evening's supper (a very serious conference) the necessary cases were opened, the tins extracted, then closed again. I still have the food lists, and it might be interesting to note the contents of one case at random, weighing 60 lb.: 4 tins sausages, 2 pineapple, 4 bacon, 5-lb. tin powdered milk, 5-lb. tin cooking fat, 2 tins pears, 2 tins peaches, 1 tin biscuits, 2 tins curry powder, 4 tins herrings.

We curried everything we could, even to eggs, to make them taste hotter, and had with us a liberal supply of the hottest chile concoctions available even in Calcutta.

Behind the march was the undercurrent of excitement that goes with the quest for information an enemy is trying to keep secret. (I was already so identified with Tibet's cause that I automatically thought of China as the "enemy".) Despite the careful arrangements and the promise that we could make contact, it became increasingly clear as we made our way across the Himalayas that the Chinese were now operating virtually all along the Nepal border. Where the passes were too high for them to live, they sent out regular patrols. They had spotter aircraft, and for sixteen days we lived in considerable doubt as to whether we could even arrive at the chosen spot and, if so, whether we should have to return to Katmandu with our mission uncompleted.

There are five main passes from Tibet into Nepal; the Tinkar Lipu, 16,000 feet; the Mane Pass, about the same height; Rasuagarhi, directly north of Katmandu; Kodari, about 8,000 feet; and the Nangpala at 19,000 feet.

All are manned by Chinese, or visited frequently by Tibetans who could cross the frontier at will and without formalities. The pass chosen for us was a little-known one north of Jumbesi, the main village—if one can call it a village—for which we were making, and a good twelve days' march from Katmandu. Jumbesi is an important village on the way to Namche Bazar, though one must not be misled by the term "village" for it contained no shops of any sort, and indeed the nearest tobacconist was two days' march away.

For day after day we marched on, up or down but never horizontally, for we were marching across the grain of the Himalayas and could rarely make a long traverse. Our coolies presented no serious problems. They could easily carry their loads, plus all sorts of things they decided to carry for themselves. We had stuck to "regulars" who knew the route well, though at Katmandu small boys had offered to hire themselves out as "half a porter" willing to carry 30 lb., while some stalwarts begged to be hired as "two coolies" ready to carry 120 lb.

The only porter trouble we had was with the one woman, a handsome, rosy-cheeked girl of twenty-one or twenty-two who carried her 60 lb. easily, but after a few days came to me complaining of severe stomach pains. I looked up the list of instructions given to me by the Westminster Hospital and promptly dosed her with chlorodyne. This seemed to satisfy her, but the next day she was back again for more, which I gave her. After a few days of this I suddenly became suspicious. She had no husband with her, but one old man with long, braided hair turned out to be her father, and with Ang Tsering acting as interpreter in my tent, and the father there to be sure there was no gossip, I gave her a very cursory examination—but quite enough to discover that she was seven months pregnant. By then we had eaten 60 lb. of food so we were able to pay her off with a good tip, and she set off cheerfully to walk home alone—a journey of eight days—to have her baby.

But on the whole each day was like the last and the next, and very much like this one, December 11, taken from my diary:

"A real stinker. Climbed steadily from 8 a.m. to 2.45 with 20 minutes off for lunch. Lost our way once but when in doubt we always take path that goes upwards. Fortunately found tracks of Ang Tsering's boots to follow. Noticed five eagles circling *below* us at lunch-time. Ate lunch under shade of giant banyan and pipal trees. Banyan, with roots hanging like skeins of wool from branches, is the male fig tree, and pipal with leaves, which (I think it was) Beverley Nichols described as like dripping green paint, is the female. Lunch consisted tin each of herrings in tomato sauce, two oranges and diluted bottled lemonade from water-bottle which we make each night with boiling water, use as hot-water-bottle when creeping into our bags but which is ice cold when we want to drink it following day. Odd to notice at this height sudden clump of poinsettias, then down below river from which we have climbed steadily for hours, wonderful scenery—at one moment we could see valley and river-bed thousands of feet below, otherwise mostly heavy clouds below us but with fabulous mountains. Came to the pass, 14,000 feet, around noon. Bits of rag hanging from sticks at top of pass. 'Sympathetic magic'—the true Buddhists tear off strips of their clothes and believe that by offering them to Buddha at the pass they are giving a part of themselves and so are throwing away part of their tiredness. Which is why they always appear at the top of a mountain. Bought some local radishes, very good, each one three feet long. We are camping tonight in hollow at 12,000 feet. Very low damp clouds boiling up into weird shapes over the peaks, moving like demons. Am writing this in my tent in two sleeping-bags. Washed one third of my body today—that's the easiest way, put my tin bowl in my tent, use it as a bidet, wash my feet one day, middle bit the next, top part the third. Fish cakes for supper, then whisky and boiled water."

Other days did not pass so uneventfully as this. One night we camped in the courtyard of a Buddhist temple alive with fluttering prayer flags. It rained heavily that evening, and as dawn broke worshippers padded past my small green tent to the temple, and a sonorous gong dismissed the night. I could hear them chanting as I drank my "bed tea". I peeped out of the tent flap; more worshippers came past, automatically spinning the prayer wheels as they entered the temple. A few minutes later, as I was washing, everything started to shake violently. The worshippers dashed out helter-skelter, flying to open ground. My toothbrush, soap and hairbrush were thrown on to the ground by unseen hands. The water in my tin bowl spilt over. I should say the earthquake lasted for perhaps thirty seconds, but it seemed a long, long time, like the moment of eternity it takes as you listen to the swish of a bomb before it explodes.

This earthquake was taken as a bad omen, for that day we had to climb to 13,000 feet to a pass known locally as "The Evil One" where three coolies had perished in snow recently. Our porters' nervousness was increased because the narrow path sliced through a heavily-wooded mountain notorious for its bandits, but we marched in close formation without any incident.

This day, I remember, had some unpleasant climbing moments for me, though there was never any danger, and to the Hillarys and Hunts of this world our journey was nothing. But I hated those narrow ledges at great heights, and in fact without Ralph I doubt whether I would ever have finished the journey. Ralph, though, regarded them as unconcernedly as if he were walking down the Strand. In some particularly precarious spot he would stop, teeter nonchalantly on the edge and, looking thousands of feet down a sheer precipice, would murmur, "Rather fine view, don't you think?" while I gulped and closed my eyes.

But it was not all like this and in fact the scenery changed astonishingly from day to day. For hours on end entire mountainsides were terraced by the assiduous Nepalis, scratching a living from the last possible inch of ground. Each one of the thousands of tiny terraces, forming steps up the mountainside, was used for grain or rice. The hillsides were dotted with neat white houses, and occasionally we would come on a large prosperous farm with stacks of corn, and the eaves cluttered with cobs for the chickens in cold weather. They looked as rich and comfortable as the big farms in the Swiss mountains, and yet here they were days from the nearest village, hours from the nearest neighbour, their "main road" being a mountain track between Namche Bazar and Katmandu. What did they do with their spare time, these isolated families? It was hard to find out. We had a job to do, and little time to spare, but when on occasion we stopped perhaps for a bite of lunch by some handsome farm, the girls vanished immediately, scurrying away like frightened hens; and the men and the countless children then formed a grave circle around us and without a word watched us eat our tinned sardines or corned beef, watching with anxious eyes for any empty tins that would be left when our brief meal was over.

They were curious and self-contained, the lives of these lonely people, for though they were self-sufficient (the only women who didn't run away were those spinning cloth) and though they had no contact with the outside world, yet they were on a road along which passed great caravans, and which hundreds of foreigners, with their thousands of porters, used on the way to Everest. Yet the local people were perhaps half a day's march or more from their nearest neighbour, and the majority of them, so far as I could discover, had never been as far even as Katmandu. It was rather like coming across a succession of hermits on the Great North Road, interested in the passing traffic, but not concerned with finding out why it was there, or where it was going.

Sometimes the farms were at great heights, but the bigger ones—and certainly the prosperous ones—were in the semi-tropical valleys through which we passed from time to time. In these we bought oranges (four shillings for seven dozen), eggs, bananas and even an occasional chicken; while monkeys watched us from a respectful distance. But even here there were problems. At one camp a farmer and his family were feverishly building a stone trap for panthers that had been worrying the flocks, and that night a live sheep was tied inside as bait and, as though it knew its fate, bleated so plaintively all night that it was impossible to sleep. We kept the camp-fire alight until dawn.

Only once in the thirty days we marched (including the return journey) did we come to a village large enough to have a shop. This was a place with the improbable name of Those (pronounced Toe-zay) in the lee of a large mountain from which the Nepalese extract iron for their terrifying swinging chain bridges over which we had to cross narrow ravines at regular intervals. These bridges, sometimes a hundred feet above a river at the bottom of a cleft, frightened me beyond anything else; and always at the back of my mind as I crossed one was the knowledge that I would have to cross it on the way back. Thick links of local Those iron held thin strands of the same metal on which were laid narrow planks. This primitive bridge swung with every movement a man made on it.

At Those we halted for a day's rest in a field on the edge of the village, and all the porters got really drunk on *chung*. Ralph distributed to each one an advance in pay, which these men, who were carrying 60 lb. over the roughest mountain tracks in the world, promptly spent on buying large bars of iron to sell in future villages. Some of them bought six, each one certainly weighing between 5 and 10 lb. and cheerfully set off the next morning with a hangover and an extra 30 or 40 lb. of weight on their backs.

Despite a lot of minor ailments among the porters, we were fortunately free from any serious trouble until we were crossing a narrow mountain stream near Jumbesi. It was not a particularly bad crossing, and most of the coolies had nimbly crossed by the loose stones in the river bed, but then one slipped. The river was moving very swiftly. As he fell his load slipped from his back and smashed open. Everything from exposed film to tins of food went swirling away before our eyes. But, even worse, as he tried to break his fall the coolie cracked down with all his force on his left arm. It snapped like a twig—at least eight days from the nearest doctor.

Ralph and I were a little behind the main stream—it was always more convenient to let the porters go ahead or behind—and when we came to the river the porter was lying groaning and squirming on the ground. One look at the arm was enough. We broke open another wooden case and Adjeeba with his kukri sliced through the wood like butter to make splints which we wrapped in cotton wool. Neither of us being doctors, we had to do the best we could. I gave him an enormous tot of rum from the medical chest, then three codeine tablets. Then I tried to straighten the boy's arm out as painlessly as possible, while Ralph applied the splints, which we tied on with strips of towel. We used another towel as a sling. There was nothing else we could do. I gave the boy a liberal supply of codeine tablets for each day and two nembutals for each night, and made preparations for his return to Katmandu with a chit to the local hospital to admit him on promise of payment from us when we returned. (Without such a chit he would probably have been kept waiting for a month for admission.)

After that there was nothing to do but send him back, an eight-day march if he moved quickly, to Katmandu. This we did, sending another porter to keep him company, distributing the load among the others.

Then we pushed on to Solar Khumbu and turned north into the great mountains and the frontier of the secret land.

This was the moment for which we had been working (and walking) so long. The scenery changed. We left the trim peasant huts behind us, and soon there were very few trees to be seen. As we climbed, the country became more ragged, the bushes more stunted, the paths narrower. The great white mountains were straight ahead, sometimes visible, sometimes hidden by cloud, and on one magnificent day, I remember, we made a long traverse with, straight ahead of us, an enormous belt of cloud blotting out the horizon, but jutting out of it, like a Japanese print, a dozen white peaks against a vivid blue sky, looking as though they were resting on cotton wool. It was an unforgettable sight.

We were now very close to the frontier, and I found it

impossible to contain my excitement. After a stiff climb we descended for half a day into a little valley which we reached on the last night. It looked for all the world like a small dell in Switzerland. As we clambered down the rocky road, slithering through mountain streams, sometimes ankle-deep in mud, taking the weight of our bodies on our picks, we saw a few white or brown huts, a couple of old men ploughing with oxen. Soon some kiddies were running out to meet us.

I was watching out for one particular landmark—a narrow bridge with a steep wooden roof that spanned the small mountain river we had been following for some hours. Less than half a day's march away from the bridge was the frontier, the pass being guarded by a patrol of Nepalese, whom we preferred not to encounter; and across this pass our friends the Tibetans could come and go more or less as they wished. Here we were supposed to meet Dondub.

Sure enough, there was the bridge, just as I had been told, and near it a camp of ragged Tibetans.

Pemba had gone ahead and our tents were already pitched when we arrived at the cluster of farms. It was a beautiful little spot, on a terraced hillside. Ralph had his tent on one terrace, I had the one a foot or so below. The small swiftly-running mountain river was so incredibly cold you could not even dip your feet in it. (But how good the water would have tasted with our evening drinks if only we had not had to boil it.) A hundred yards below the camp was the wooden bridge.

Tea was ready and the rum bottle was out as we sat down in our chairs and pulled off our boots and stretched our toes. Adjeeba brought me a bowl of hot water to wash my feet in. The Sherpas and porters were foraging for wood. It was utterly peaceful and almost impossible to believe that round the corner war was raging.

The actual encounter with Dondub was almost an anti-climax. Ralph and I were opening food-cases for the evening meal when a beggar came over from the near-by camp. He was the filthiest-looking man I have ever seen and it was a miracle how his rags still clung to him. He came in, rested on his staff, asked for alms, and then I heard the word "Dondub" and knew immediately that this was the man.

After that it was only a question of interpreting, and long before sunset Dondub was on his way back to Tibet to tell the general that we had arrived.

Tobgye Wangdue arrived the following evening. His small party of nine men, including Dondub, came walking down the narrow path of the mountain facing our camp. Others followed in the next few days, all of them leaving their horses behind in Tibet and marching the short distance from the frontier pass.

The general was a massive man, at least six feet tall, with a back as straight as a plank of wood. His scarred head was shaven so that old cuts made his bald pate look like a football. He wore neither beard nor moustaches, and I was told that he shaved his head daily. In the belt of his sheepskin tunic he carried a sword, a pistol and a kukri, and he had a rifle slung across his back. He could speak no English, neither could his followers, but Dondub, the man disguised as a beggar who was awaiting us, spoke a little, and we had our Sherpas.

It was three days before Christmas, a bright, cold day, when the Khamba leader walked into our camp and for the first time somebody from the outside world heard the frightful story of China's war of extermination behind the white barrier of the Himalayas.

VII

TIBET UNDER CONQUEST

The picture unfolded to us in that small camp in the Himalayas was grimmer than anything I had imagined. But so was the picture of heroic resistance. By now, according to Wangdue, there were 750,000 Red Chinese troops in the country, including 300,000 moved in during 1958; 4,500,000 colonisers, including women and children, had been sent in from China. A "police army" of 3,000 now controlled civic duties in all major cities and towns. All were doing regular training with Chinese combat troops, and all were armed. Clutching desperately at any hope of preserving his diminishing authority the Dalai Lama was virtually a prisoner of the Chinese in the Potala, and being subjected daily to more and more insults. The guerrillas claimed to have killed 50,000 Chinese in 1958, whilst admitting they had lost 22,000 dead. The whole story was like flicking over the pages of Dante's *Inferno*: monasteries bombed, monks shot at prayer, old Tibetans used as slaves, Tibetans themselves killing their wives before taking to the mountains to fight, as all Tibetan women were being forced to bear at least one "Chinese" child.

Thousands of Tibetan boys and girls had been drafted into mass education schools in China; starvation was an ever-present threat and nobody could even guess the number who had died from it. As the fighting increased, the Chinese were stepping up punitive raids and bombing attacks, and, according to the guerrillas, 17,000 Tibetans other than freedom fighters had been killed in these measures. By the turn of 1958 the Chinese had seven major airfields completed in Tibet —at Tachienlu, Nagchuka, Gartok, Lhasa, Chamdo, Kanoe, and Litang. As the Chinese drove inwards and southwards, a labour force of 420,000 Chinese women coolies had already built six major roads—three from China inwards, three pointing at or parallel to India's northern frontiers. Along them the Chinese had installed a complete network of spy stations.

Against this the warrior tribe of Tibet, the Khambas, was fighting to the death, but as Wangdue admitted, "We have no hope any more, but we shall fight to the death for our honour and because we are tied by unbreakable bonds to our religious institutions which are more important to us than life."

This terrible story, and the details which follow, we learned not only from the general, but from his followers, and from the wounded who came to our camp to be treated.

The fascinating aspect of all this (though we did not know it then) was that if anybody in the West had suggested at Christmas 1958 that the Dalai Lama would be forced to flee Lhasa a bare three months later, he would have been taken for an alarmist.

Yet at the very time I was talking to the guerrilla leaders on the Tibetan frontier, the forces and strains inside the country were already shaping the Dalai Lama's destiny more swiftly than anybody imagined. Indeed, the situation could not have materially changed before the great revolt in Lhasa in March, and so the picture which Tobgye Wangdue and his colleagues gave us was very much the picture in Tibet at the moment of the Dalai Lama's escape. It was a picture that emphasised again and again China's utter determination to destroy everything that in the past had made Tibet a country unique in the world. Ruthlessly Red China was changing the age-old culture of the country and doing everything possible to stamp out its deeply-rooted religious institutions. At first it seemed that the Chinese left the Tibetan Lamas alone, but when they discovered that the guerrillas had obtained arms from some of the monasteries—from time immemorial the arms caches have been stored in the monasteries—they started punitive attacks on the places of worship in an endeavour to terrorise the monks into refusing

help for the guerrillas. Four of the country's most important
Lamas had been imprisoned or perhaps had been killed; it
was impossible to know, since they had disappeared. These
men were Kathok Sithu, Dho Trupchen, Zogchen Premarig-
zing, and Shakeldon Gyatsho. Eight monasteries had been
deliberately destroyed by bombing and many of their priests
murdered after Khamba activity in their areas. Buddhist
images had been desecrated and Tibetan books burned. The
famous Lithang Gonchen monastery, founded by the third
Dalai Lama, was razed and its eighty-year-old abbot and
four other priests were killed after Chinese troops had
sprayed the massive figure of Buddha with tommy-guns.

Behind the story of day-to-day violence lay the threat of
famine. Tibet used to be self-sufficient but, with more than
5,000,000 Chinese living off the land, they were by now in
desperate trouble. The Chinese had looted all the ancient
granaries, where for centuries Tibet had stored grain against
years of famine. Food prices were twenty times higher than
seven years ago. The Chinese had started food rationing,
but a coupon for a day's food—even if it could be honoured—
gave a Tibetan peasant, who no longer had any land, one-
fifth of what he ate (and that was not much) before the
Chinese invasion.

The Tibetan grazing grounds and small plots had been
taken over for Chinese colonisers, who moved into villages
as complete units, ejecting every Tibetan. Hundreds of
Tibetan villages no longer had a single Tibetan in them.
The women had been killed, the men had fled to the hills.
As they moved in, the Chinese used the old Communist trick
of dividing families. Over the years, 20,000 children had
been taken to China for "education" and many were now
back with no knowledge of life other than as it is lived in Red
China, so son and daughter were informing against father
and mother as the children returned with Chinese propaganda films, Chinese books, to take up posts teaching the
new young of Tibet.

Though Tibetan guerrillas were operating on a large
scale it was difficult to assess their effectiveness. The

Tibetan horsemen, who reported seeing Russians with the Chinese
troops

Khamba tribesmen, who are at the core of Tibetan resistance against
the Chinese Communists

A typical rock path, showing the sort of country through which the Dalai Lama had to travel

Traverse approaching "Windy Corner"

guerrillas insisted that several radio sets had been parachuted to them by Chiang Kai-shek, though it was impossible to confirm this. On the other hand, there was no doubt that the guerrillas were seriously harassing the Chinese, and in many areas had forced the Chinese to supply their far-flung garrisons by air, as all their patrols were ambushed.

The Chinese had been forced to make another link on their biggest road from China to Lhasa after the Tibetans blew up key bridges over the mountain passes. The guerrillas had also forced the Chinese to bring in heavy troop concentrations to small but strategic villages like Tingri, just across the border from Everest.

But more and more the Tibetans were concentrating in an area which emphasised the most critical aspect of this forgotten war that affected us in the West—the roads that lead southwards or are parallel to the northern borders of India or the Indian States. Nowhere was the southward drive more apparent than in the massive programme of road construction which the Tibetans were harassing. Often these were being built under Russian supervision—and how the Russians there must have been chuckling as they remembered Lenin's famous dictum: "The way to Paris lies through Peking and Calcutta."

Just north of our camp a great new road was all but completed from Shigatse to the border of Kashmir. It followed the River Tsangpo west, near the Nepal border, through Saka and Tradom, where the garrison had been increased to 3,000 Chinese troops following big guerrilla attacks.

The road was almost finished, and after Tradom led to Gartok, a big trading centre where the Chinese had an airfield and more than 4,000 men, and the last stretch is probably completed by now, linking Gartok to Rudok, near the Kashmir border. Another road from Lhasa links up with this one at Shigatse and strikes south through Gyangtse right to the Sikkim border. Ten thousand guerrillas were constantly patrolling this last route, blowing up any convoys they could ambush.

Against this massive Chinese military programme, the

F

Khambas were fighting in their tens of thousands, and it is easier now than it was on the border to realise how inevitable it was that this fighting should swell into open revolt in Lhasa itself. The astonishing factor is the speed with which the fighting intensified. When we were talking to the guerrilla leaders, my general impression was that, however widespread the fighting, it still consisted of many pockets of resistance to the Chinese rather than a general concerted plan; and it was hard to believe that in such a short time the Khambas, incensed by Chinese punitive measures, would be strong enough to march on Lhasa, stage an open war in the streets of the city itself while the Dalai Lama was being smuggled out on the escape route to India.

It was all the more incredible because reports varied about the quantity and quality of the guerrilla's arms, though I am inclined to believe that they were (and still are) much better than is generally supposed. There is no doubt that tens of thousands of guns poured into Tibet during and after the fall of the Chinese Nationalistic Government, sold mainly by gun-running generals suddenly out of work. George Patterson said that while travelling in Tibet "I saw every type of modern rifle being used with deadly accuracy by almost every Tibetan over twenty years of age". Patterson was sure that in the past few years sporadic supplies had been dropped to the guerrillas from aircraft with Chinese markings, so perhaps it was indeed true that they also had radio sets sent by Chiang Kai-shek.

But even if the Khambas had arms, they were woefully short of ammunition. They had almost nothing to stand up to China's modern artillery and tanks except, ironically, precipitous mountain walls, snowbound passes, desert and an appalling climate. It was this which made them, in the words of one of our informants, "fight to the death with the knife". Early in December the guerrillas fought two fierce battles, typical of the fighting that was slowly spreading across the whole of Tibet.

At the town of Nimo Kharkhang, south-west of Gyangtse, 600 Chinese were killed in a pitched battle when 700 guerril-

las made a night attack on Chinese reinforcements relieving
the garrison of 1,500 men on the edge of the town. To save
bullets, Tibetans fought with knives. Half the Chinese escaped to the hills, and, as usual, no prisoners were taken on
either side. The Tibetan losses, mostly from machine-gun
fire, were put at 350.

The other battle was at Yukok between Lhasa and
Shigatse, where guerrillas made a dawn attack on a Chinese
convoy. In much the same way as the rebels operated in
North Africa, the guerrillas during the night dug trenches
across the dirt mountain road in a defile near the edge of
Yukok, a sprawling, straggling, trading centre. At 6.30 a.m.,
as nine Chinese lorries drove through the narrow mountain
pass and were stopped by the trenches, Tibetans opened with
rifle fire. Three hundred Chinese and 200 Tibetans were
killed in an action lasting an hour and a half. To the six-
foot Khambas, battles like these were everyday affairs.
Coming from the east, a disputed area between China and
Tibet long before the invasion, they are natural-born
brigands, whose fathers before them fought the Chinese in
sporadic raids. Now they were bringing their swashbuckling
tactics to the west of Tibet and the southern approaches to
India, and my information was that at least 20,000 Khambas
were fighting desperately in an area north of Nepal and
south of the river Tsangpo bounded on the west by the same
longitude as Katmandu, and to the east by a north-south
line between Lhasa and Gyangtse. They were operating
mostly in groups of two to three hundred men under a
central command, so that the groups could join up for big
attacks. Almost all had been fighting since 1952, and had
been driven westwards by the Chinese. Though ammunition
was reportedly running very short, nobody really knew the
number of guns and bullets still hidden in the big monasteries
of Tibet, the traditional storehouses of weapons, but they
must have been large, for some of these monasteries are
cities in themselves, like Drepung, three miles from Lhasa,
which has—or had—a permanent population of 8,000 monks.

I was told of one instance where one monastery alone

furnished guerrillas with 2,000 rifles. On several occasions the total force of all guerrillas in Tibet was variously put at between 80,000 and 150,000. Probably the former figure is nearer the mark. This included large contingents to the north and also east of Lhasa, and probably also included peasants who had been robbed of their grazing lands by Chinese colonisers, and were becoming "part-time" freedom fighters.

Most of the Chinese garrisons north of Nepal were small and were being supplied by air-drop, as Khambas harassed any convoy and also regularly blew up the make-shift bridges that took weeks to repair and without which nobody could cross from one mountain to another. The air-drop provided the Khambas with their favourite battle; they could spot the plane as quickly as the Chinese in their forts, and they waited right under the noses of the Chinese for the parachutes to float down. Time after time they captured them, as the Chinese apparently were not very accurate, and the Chinese dared not venture too far from their forts. It must have been an incredible sight to see hundreds, if not thousands, of Khambas arrive on the scene of battle and just camp there—a few yards out of rifle range —in full view of the enemy, their tiny fires burning all night like a set piece for a medieval battle in a film.

By the end of 1958 the Khambas even had their own courts where they tried Tibetan quislings. Any Tibetans found dealing with the enemy received a minimum sentence of forty lashes with a yakhide whip; second offences were punished by death. The Khambas were utterly ruthless with Tibetans who refused to help them. "This is your war we are fighting," they said, and as one of their most urgent needs was for horses, they insisted on changing their tired mounts for fresh ones commandeered from local Tibetans.

They expected food if the local population had any, particularly yak milk, which they made into hard cheese. Each man carried enough "iron rations" to last a month: *champa*, the bread of Tibet, made of roasted barley meal with yak milk, or dried meat, which in Tibet lasts for up to three years and tastes rather like the hard blood-red smoked meat the peasants keep for months in the Grison mountains of Switzerland. The Khambas all wore the same uniform, consisting of a roughly-dried sheepskin, with the wool on the inside, which was tucked up around the middle by a large belt forming a sort of blouse and skirt. At nightfall all they did was take off the belt and the garment became a night-shirt. Even at the time of the year when we were there, they automatically dossed down on the ground without tents.

But what struck me most was their cheerful acceptance of the inevitable. The Khambas can never win. For every Chinese they kill, Peking can send in ten more. But the Khambas had reached the stage where they were fighting not for their lives any more but for something deeper and more fundamental—for their God and their way of life, however primitive it may appear to people of the West.

Almost ten years ago (October 25, 1950) I cut out an article by Norman Cliff in the *News Chronicle* and I have kept it to this day; for long before the Khamba revolt started, he told simply the reasons why it would one day have to come:

"The Communists propose to 'liberate' the Tibetans, who have guarded their independence so jealously against foreign influence that all talk of Anglo-American imperialist domination is the rankest nonsense.

"Presumably the Tibetans are to be 'liberated' from priestly control, from the opium of religion and from slavery to a feudal landed aristocracy.

"Can it be wondered that they have made no demand to exchange the consolations of their modified form of Buddhism for the mental shackles of Communism or the tyranny of landlords for the dictates of commissars and secret police?

"In a world torn by conflict every island of peace needs to be preserved. Tibet is one of the few still left.

"What have these sturdy, cheerful folk to learn from the war-ridden outside world? Far from primitive, they can boast of magnificent architecture, inspired religious sculpture, exquisite tapestries, handsome hand-produced books, gaily artistic ornaments, colourful dancing, expressive music and a rich and extensive folk-lore. Tibet has preferred to exist without benefit of industrialisation or mechanisation. Only the things of the mind and of the spirit are regarded as of lasting importance."

This, then, was the situation at the beginning of 1959; one in which ferocious fighting by ill-equipped guerrillas was spreading over the whole of this barren country and, as inevitably happens, was provoking increasing reprisals by the Chinese. So far, no word of this had really reached the outside world; but it was clear that such an explosive state of affairs could not continue without some even greater act of drama. The Chinese could not allow the Khambas to increase their power and sway over the Tibetan masses and the Government of Lhasa; and, on the other hand, the Khambas, with reduced supplies and weapons and a heavy death-roll, could not go on indefinitely.

So though the fighting continued as fiercely as ever—and indeed was shortly to mount in intensity and ferocity—more and more political pressures were brought to bear on the Dalai Lama and his immediate advisers by those Lamas who had whole-heartedly thrown in their lot with the Khambas. Throughout the fighting, the Dalai Lama had shown an astonishing combination of firmness and wisdom for a man whose birth and parentage were of the humblest, and who, unless one believes in his reincarnation, was in fact quite unsuited to the task of international politics that he had never been expected to undertake. With great restraint he had done everything to keep his country, and his religion, as nearly independent as possible. He had two years before appealed to India for sanctuary and help, only to be persuaded by a hypocritical Nehru to accept vague assurances from India and China which were never kept; Nehru, in those two vital years since the 1956 uprising, could easily have used his influence to persuade the Chinese to moderate their attitude, and some sort of compromise might easily have been reached by negotiations. But Nehru is nothing if not thorough, and the hero of Kashmir did not even choose to express his sympathy or concern to his neighbour Tibet over China's default.

So, as the Khamba revolt intensified, Tibetan volunteers who felt they were being used as pawns by the equally cynical powers of India and China, were more and more in the frame of mind to believe that politically, even more than militarily, something drastic had to be done. All their pleas for world help had been in vain. All their cries remained unanswered. If the Tibetans did not act, then most assuredly the Chinese would.

VIII

TRAINING FOR CHINESE COLONISTS

During the days with the Tibetans I learned a great deal more about what was happening in Tibet than most Europeans; particularly about one aspect which interested me—the problems facing Nehru, both ideological and practical.

Nehru's timidity over Tibet appeared to be the result of fear or a genuine preference for the Communist *bloc*, or a mixture of both (I shall have more to say about this in a later chapter). But it was quite clear that Nehru was facing very serious infiltration along his northern frontiers, and was doing nothing about it. Nehru is not the first timid man to believe that sycophantic overtures to totalitarian régimes ensure genuine friendship. Even now, Nehru shows no signs of any change in his intention to maintain towards China the conciliatory attitude outwardly based on "panch shila" (the "five principles of coexistence and non-interference" which originally appeared in the Sino–Indian Treaty on Tibet of 1954). But thinking Indians are certainly perturbed about recent trends along the Himalayan frontiers for several reasons. Firstly, there is China's continued, though passive, claims to suzerainty over Bhutan and to a large part of northern Assam. Both these areas repeatedly appear as Chinese on new maps published in Peking. When Nehru was recently questioned about these maps in the Indian parliament, even he referred sarcastically to the Chinese leaders' "speed in revising everything except their maps".

I found intelligent Indians deeply concerned about the impact on the hill peoples of Chinese propaganda claims about rapid progress among their cousins in Tibet, which increased their dissatisfaction with what the Indian Government was doing to help them, and had been the cause of much dissension in the Himalayan states.

Discontent among the hill peoples in Indian territory or in India's protected states had broken out into armed rebellion only in the Naga Hills in Assam, where very many hundreds of people have now been killed and the army is still unable to pin down the elusive rebels. But there is widespread unrest in other hill areas, ranging from Garwhal, west of Nepal, where traders have seen their customary links with Tibet cut by the Chinese, and blame Delhi for not providing them with an alternative livelihood, to Sikkim, Bhutan, and various Assam districts. Not all the unrest arises from Chinese propaganda or from the hillmen's traditional distrust of Indians from the plains. There are also local frictions.

In both Bhutan and Sikkim, a certain rivalry has been developing between Nepalese, Tibetans, and local peoples such as the Lepchas. Bhutan is orientated towards Buddhist Tibet, but its people also feel some pressure from Hindu Nepal. In Sikkim, Nepalese have settled in such numbers that they now form three-quarters of the population. There has been some agitation for the creation of a "greater Nepal", which would take in Sikkim and other Himalayan areas, such as the Darjeeling district, where Nepalese have settled in large numbers.

At the same time, the Tibetans' struggle against Chinese Communist rule has spilt over into Indian territory and introduced one more dangerous element into the borderlands. I found the Tibetan rebels' resentment was now directed against Delhi as well as against Peking, because they regarded the 1954 agreement on Tibet as a betrayal, and also felt that several appeals for help, or at least sympathy, to the Indian Government, had brought neither reply nor acknowledgement. Privately, Delhi gave them the unpalatable advice to try Gandhian non-violence against the Communists, and they could not forget that the Dalai Lama asked for sanctuary in India in January 1957, but was rebuffed.

The presence of large numbers of anti-Indian Tibetans in the Indian borderlands (particularly in Sikkim and northern Bengal) gave the Chinese an excellent excuse for manning their side of the frontier and, even more, organising an intensive spy network directed to India and the border states to foment the dissatisfaction already apparent and to prepare the way at leisure for any large-scale Chinese movement southwards.

Since there is no knowing what further steps the Chinese have taken in the months between writing and publishing this volume, this is the picture as it appeared at the start of 1959, and as it was given to me by the guerrilla leaders at the border. It was frightening enough.

As Red China's "interest" in India became daily more evident, the Chinese were mapping all the border areas, training pseudo-traders by the thousand to infiltrate south of Tibet. They had started special language classes in Nepali, Hindi and Bengali, with at least fifty Russians working with them instituting training systems sometimes within a few miles of the borders.

Under names like "Commercial Academy" and "Border Affairs Office" the Chinese had an espionage system that was running like clockwork, turning out thousands of fifth columnists a year.

To us of the West, watching the oozing spread of Chinese Communism, this was perhaps the most sinister story to come out of Tibet, for it proved beyond all doubt that deep down the invasion and occupation of Tibet were only stepping-stones to further conquests in the future.

In Lhasa was the headquarters of the Tibetan "Commercial Academy", which had a special class devoted to "civil intelligence". When I was on the frontier, eight classes were running concurrently, each with eighty members who were enrolled for six months. Nearly all students were either Chinese from the disputed area of East Tibet or Tibetans coerced to join. They were taught elementary trading techniques so that they could pass the frontier.

After finishing at the "Commercial Academy" students were sent to one of three "Infiltration Training Academies". One was the "India Infiltration Class" where almost all students were Chinese College Graduates speaking some English. Most of the instructors were Chinese or Russian with experience of India. Each class had fifty students, with a course lasting a year. They were being taught Indian dialects, the English language, with four hours a day devoted to intelligence work. As they graduated they were being sent to India either as merchants or members of missions. The second class was the "Nepal Infiltration Class", which at the beginning of 1959 was training 200 Chinese and 100 Nepalis (who had crossed into Tibet). The school was in Lhasa. The third class was for students who would go into Bhutan and Sikkim, and was composed of about a hundred students. As Tibetans, Sikkimese and Bhutanese have similar features and languages, their training for infiltration was comparatively easy. From all these three training schools men were pouring across the border either as traders or often disguised as monks.

Entirely different but equally sinister was the work of the "Border Affairs Office". This office was located in an isolated building near the headquarters of the Chinese Army in Lhasa and it had three advanced offices.

The most important was located at a township called Chung Petan in a steep valley in the Himalayas between Tibet and Sikkim about twenty miles from Gangtok. Here five intelligence officers from Peking, with eighty Chinese already experienced in fifth-column work, were living, supported by 150 members of the "Police Army". The headquarters of the Chinese 154th regiment was situated at near-by Yatung and the main duties of the office were to train young Tibetans recently returned from China to become pseudo-traders so they could enter Sikkim and Kalimpong. They were also mapping every inch of the border country, and from the mountain area of Chung Petan could actually see almost as far as Gangtok, the capital of Sikkim.

The second big office was at the township of Nelammo, north of Everest and close to the Nepalese border. Three Russians were stated to be working there. A third office was in the town of Tsona Dzong, north of Tawang, where the Dalai was soon to stay.

In addition the Chinese in Tibet had started a "Border Survey Column", in which more than 300 Chinese mapping experts were working on the disputed areas along the borders of Tibet and Nepal, Bhutan, Sikkim, and Kashmir.

I do not for a moment suggest that all this activity on the Indian border suggests an invasion by the Chinese in the immediate future. But I do suggest that it is not being done for nothing. India is at the moment in a mess—fundamentally, economically, socially—and Nehru is going to die one day. Being India, his death might cause a giant uprising, though nobody can prophesy with accuracy; certainly, however, post-Nehru India will be very different from the India of today. The Chinese, by means of an efficient spy system based on Tibet, are sowing the seeds of dissension on which Communism thrives so well.

Who knows what the future holds? Personally I believe that no totalitarian régime can flourish without aggrandisement, and I really believe that China definitely sees India as a victim for aggression—political aggression at least. Certainly if a world war were to break out, China would, through the conquest of Tibet, march straight into India.

It was General Wang Tsen, head of the Chinese Army in 1950, who made one of Communism's biggest gaffs when publicly, if thoughtlessly, he announced "between Peking and Delhi there is no large river. We can approach Delhi easily through Kashmir". The last stretch of road to carry the Chinese Army to the Kashmir border is now all but completed, the link in the far west of Tibet from Gartok to Rudok.

Is it possible that the occupation of Tibet by Red China is just a beginning, just a prologue to a mighty thrust southwards or westwards that will engulf us all? One must, I suppose, discount some of the insistence of the Tibetan guerrillas that this is so, for as they continue to fight a losing battle their only hope of help is to convince the West of the danger to countries outside Tibet. Yet even allowing for any exaggeration, all the evidence points to eventual aggression southwards. Why build this road from Lhasa to Kashmir— almost as long as from Lhasa to Chungking? Tibet is not, as many people think, one vast plateau behind the Himalayas. Ranges of mountains divide the country into basins. There is no way across except over the passes which are as fierce as those in Nepal.

The Rudok road is one of the modern world's most spectacular achievements, far more dramatic than China's roads of entry from the east, the only part of Tibet where access is easy. Reports say that up to 80,000 Chinese women died building this road across the world's most savage terrain and which can have absolutely no possible commercial value. Anyway, why build an airfield in far west Gartok? It, too, has no commercial value and like the road it has no military value in the present conflict with Tibet. The Chinese certainly do not need an airfield at Gartok for the subjection of the local people, for the guerrillas have never operated so far west in strength. Apart from ferrying in materials or experts for the road-building operation, Gartok airfield can have only one value—for future operations.

Communism—of whatever brand—never relies on only one method of attack, and as the Chinese build up their massive forces in Tibet, their espionage work on India's northern frontiers is already showing results among the hill peoples.

Nehru surely cannot be blind to what is happening along his northern frontier. To the Chinese his "non-interference" is a wonderful cover for their ruthless drive to establish a fifth-column in India, and not necessarily for operations in the next five, ten or twenty years, but for *some* time.

By now many thousands of Reds disguised as traders or monks have crossed into the Indian hill districts—places like Bhutan, which still has no roads and where entire districts already believe that their cousins in Tibet are better off under the Chinese than they are. The usual plausible lies about high guaranteed wages in Tibet, free education and hospitals and schools go down very well in a country like Bhutan which has never been opened up. It is foolish to scoff at this as unlikely and exaggerated. It is a classic approach that always looks exaggerated in cold print until the results begin to pay off, as one day they may well do. Penetration of this sort is a long-term task, but the Chinese are patient people and this region is perfect for sowing discontent.

As the Khamba revolution has intensified, Chinese promises of a withdrawal to the east have been hurriedly forgotten and now there are Chinese troops and permanent barrack blocks close to the Indian frontier from Kashmir to Burma.

Because of the wild country the Chinese have so far been unable to contain the Khambas, and as I write this it is clear that large parts of Tibet are still in a virtual state of open warfare. But this still does not explain entirely why Red China brought in 300,000 more troops in 1958. The guerrillas are comparatively poorly armed, drugs and ammunition are critically short, and they surely number less than 100,000. Yet China now has an occupation army of three-quarters of a million. It is all part of the build-up, like the colonisers, nearly four million of them industriously starting a new life in a country that is being erased from the map. One day there will be no more Tibet, for the Chinese are determined to exterminate the Tibetans. They are doing so with a terrible ferocity, like ants devouring everything in their path. Chinese civilians have already moved in over the corpses of the Tibetans and one day Tibet will be a province of China, not a country under military oppression, because there will be nobody left to oppress. That will be the moment of danger, when Red China, as one country inhabited by Chinese, extends from the Pacific to Kashmir.

IX

REVOLT IN LHASA

The Tibetans believe there are sixteen hells, eight hot and eight cold. The hot hells include one in which the body is cut in pieces with red-hot saws, the process being dragged out over half a million years. One cold hell is so intense it cracks the flesh and skin which is then pecked for a similar period by birds which have iron beaks. During the time we spent with the Tibetans they were regularly consigning the Chinese to one or the other with, I must say, my full support, for never was there a case in modern history of more wicked and senseless cruelty than Red China's needless murder of thousands of simple people. It was like a drunken man who comes home and thrashes his children for want of something better to do. Yet the world NSPCC (which has the shorter title of UNO) could do nothing. It was tragic, for in many ways I found the Tibetans like children in need of care and protection. They were backward but deeply contented by the simplest pleasures or gestures. A ferocious face that hides fear would break into a wonderful smile if I smiled first. Even adults would pick up an old envelope with the genuine delight of a child who could see no difference in value between a penny whistle and a bar of gold. In their very simplicity they were charming, and during the few days with them I came to know some of them well.

From the humblest refugee in tatters to the splendidly-built Khambas, all had one curious, childlike, double trait: a beautiful, enviable serenity, combined with a boisterous humour that would break out at the slightest provocation. Now that my experiences there are ended, it is hard sometimes to realise what was going on so near to us as we talked by the camp-fire; men being shot, women raped, children murdered. Our camp, pitched on its series of terraces cut into the hillside with the pretty river burbling by, became a centre for visitors and when the dark took command around six o'clock, more than a dozen fires glowed and crackled in a circle round our tents. The Tibetans hardly ever used a precious match. Callused hands grabbed for a burning ember to start a minute fire near another one. Men built up a pyramid of twigs and blew and blew until a flame was born. Supper was a rough and ready affair in which each man licked his tin plate clean just like a cat.

As the night thickened, sad low songs, possibly prayers, touched the heart like Negro spirituals. Shallow bowls of local *chung* were passed round, but by eight the camp was dead, the two of us in our warm double sleeping-bags, the Tibetans huddled in their sheepskins by the dying fires. Their clothes were shocking, but I hardly think the Chinese can be blamed for that, as many Tibetan peasants never take their clothes off—not once—until they start to drop off, when they are cut down for children.

We had two children in camp whose father had been murdered and they were dressed in a thousand patches incredibly held together. The eldest was four or five and smoked every cigarette butt he could find. The Tibetans were very fond of our cigarettes and smoked them by gripping the smoking end between the edge of the palm and their little finger and then, with the fist closed and lips pressed between thumb and forefinger, "pulled" the smoke through the intervening space. I did not mind giving them cigarettes so long as I did not have to try their tobacco, which was usually mixed with dried rhubarb.

But the most popular item out of all our stores was that good old stand-by, tinned salmon, for the Tibetans love fish but believe that the souls of departed humans enter the bodies of fish, so it is rarely included in their diet as one might be eating one's own grandmother. But as one man pointed out, "Naturally the Tibetans' souls only enter Tibetan fish, so yours is quite safe."

This practical attitude to religion cost us many a tin of

Their houses have been destroyed, their lives threatened by the Reds, but these Tibetan children face life with a smile

A ferocious face that hides fear will break into a wonderful smile if you smile first

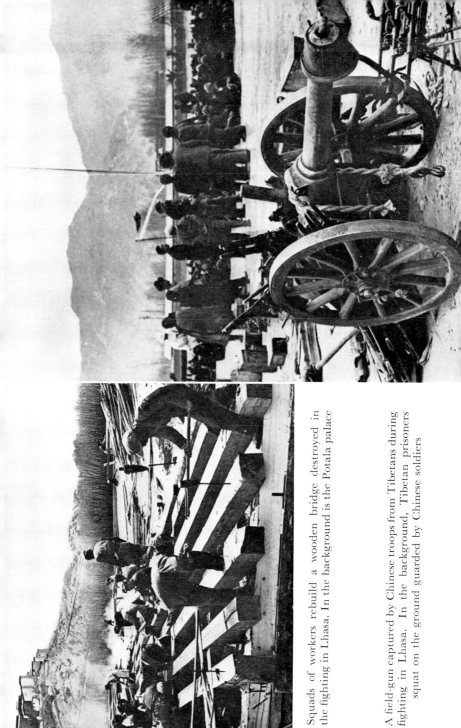

Squads of workers rebuild a wooden bridge destroyed in the fighting in Lhasa. In the background is the Potala palace

A field-gun captured by Chinese troops from Tibetans during fighting in Lhasa. In the background, Tibetan prisoners squat on the ground guarded by Chinese soldiers salmon but nothing to the quantity of medical stores we dispensed. We found the Tibetans had a sublime faith in the power of the pill—any pill—aspirin being our last resort when we did not know what to do.

Most of our cases were small wounds that had been left to fester, but more serious ones involved us in all sorts of complications. In one case where a man's shoulder had been badly cut and infected, I dressed it, but also gave him fourteen Terramycin tablets—two a day for a week. Everything was explained to the Khamba fighter and he was told to take two immediately.

Not at all. With great care he laid out fourteen stones on the ground, took twelve away, one at a time, and when only two were left looked up as though to approve of my mathematics and promptly swallowed two pills.

This I believe was because a pill is rather like a dried pea, which in Tibet stands for a unit of a hundred, and he may have thought he had to take two hundred pills a day, as I discovered when we distributed a large tin of sweets to some refugees. Symbols had to be used to divide them up—each hundred was represented by a dried pea, each ten by a splinter of wood, five by a fragment of porcelain, and each single sweet by a small stone. It took nearly a day of enormous pleasure to share out seven pounds of sweets.

But nothing staggered our Tibetan friends so much as our Christmas dinner. As a change from bully beef and tinned sausages we had carried over the mountain passes on our long journey a bottle of champagne, a haggis (the most Christmasy thing we could find in Calcutta), a plum pudding and a bottle of rum.

When the champagne cork popped, the Khambas literally jumped for their knives. The haggis in its envelope mystified them and there was a wild scramble for the casing when we tipped the contents on to our tin plates. But the *pièce de résistance* was the pudding, which Pemba had boiled for four hours. He brought it to us and we poured rum all over it. There was a gasp of fear as the pudding burst into

G

flames; it turned into a groan of wonder or fear when the two sahibs calmly started to eat "fire".

Unfortunately this Christmas dinner had to be followed by a ceremonial cup of Tibetan tea, which I do not commend as a general drink. Tea plays a highly important part in the life of every Tibetan and the average Tibetan drinks as many as forty cups of tea a day.

Near our camp was the settlement of a Tibetan family that had an air of much more permanence than our guests the Khambas, and it was arranged that we should take tea there. We found three Tibetans awaiting us—the husband, his wife and their child.

The man wore long pigtails to his waist and was dressed in a flowing robe tucked around the middle with a huge belt of scarlet and blue. His sword hung across his back in a silver scabbard and he wore felt boots up to the knees, with slits behind, and tied with strands of thick, brightly-coloured wool.

His pink-cheeked wife, who was called Tashi, went to make the tea, and we followed her inside the tent, which was made of yak hair with a hole in the centre for the fire smoke. Tea was quite a ritual. Tashi broke off some leaves and twigs of tea, which in Tibet is always pressed into bricks for convenience, and tossed them into a copper cauldron. To them she added a little wood ash to bring out the colour. Then she put in some brackish water and thoroughly boiled the mixture. Once it was boiled she strained off the liquid with a bamboo ladle and put it into a churn, adding salt and a liberal helping of butter. Fortunately she did not (as so often happens) throw in a little yak dung for good measure.

She churned it until it was thoroughly mixed, then poured the liquid, rather like soup, into an earthenware pot. We drank it from the little wooden bowls which all Tibetans carry in the folds of their gowns and which they make from growths on trees that they slice off and hollow out, the cup appropriately being called a "ba", which is Tibetan for "goitre".

If there is little to be said for a cup of Tibetan tea, there is (to be frank) even less to be said for a plate of Tibetan food. *Champa*, the bread of Tibet, was to me absolutely uneatable, and I heard many stories of serious cases of Chinese disaffection when rice was unobtainable and they were forced to eat *champa* as a staple diet. Baking is completely unknown in Tibet, and so *champa* is made of barley meal that is roasted and powdered like flour. Any meal one is unlucky enough to eat is about as unpleasant, particularly if one has seen the Tibetan way of slaughtering animals, as I had. The Tibetans are great meat eaters if they can get it, even the Lamas, though the Buddhist creed prohibits the taking of life.

To overcome this, the butchers in Tibet (and other Buddhist centres) belong to a special caste so abhorred and detested they cannot even marry outside their caste, and can have no social intercourse with any other Tibetans. They live in Tibet's most squalid houses, often built entirely from the horns of slaughtered animals, and when I saw the butchers prepare to kill some goats for a Buddhist ceremony at a lonely monastery, the Lamas came out and salved their consciences by blessing the animals and praying that they might be reborn on a higher sphere in their next life.

The butchers held the limbs of each animal to prevent struggling, then pierced the heart with a sword, giving it an extra thrust or two to make sure. Even this was not considered enough evidence of death, so after each stabbing one of the butchers thrust his arm through the hole in the body and tore the heart out.

The peace-loving Lamas loitered by, not really taking much notice of such an everyday affair, but waiting to bargain as soon as the flesh was offered for sale.

For the Khambas, living on the trail, there was virtually no meat from one month to another, for even if they raided (as they often did) farms known to be sympathetic to the Chinese, they still could not, as good Buddhists, kill the livestock on the farm, and there are few butchers except in the five or six big towns of Tibet.

Their great change from *champa* was cheese, which I found to be just as unpalatable. The family living near our camp made cheese, if somebody provided the ingredients, and one day a party of Khambas walked off and returned with about twenty gallons of yak milk (some of it slightly pink owing to bleeding ulcers in the yaks). This they took to Tashi's tent. Once it was curdled, Tashi boiled it over a fire in shallow pans, and when it was fairly cool she emptied it into small sacks from which all the liquid was pressed out. It left an unpleasant-looking spongy mass which, before it hardened, she cut into squares and threaded on strings, then hung them over a fire to smoke there. In a few days they were dark brown and as hard as iron. I tried, but it was quite impossible to bite a piece off. When the Khambas (paying for Tashi's work with some of the cheese) wanted to eat it, they either soaked it for a few hours, or usually chewed it like a plug of tobacco, a square of cheese lasting for hours.

The food situation was getting desperate by the end of 1958, for with millions of Chinese living off the inhospitable land, there had long since ceased to be enough to go round and, as one might expect, the Tibetans were always last on the list. It was hard for us to realise, with the lush valleys of Nepal below us, that in many of the high villages of Tibet, the crops never ripen, but are grown only as grass for the animals' winter fodder. It was hard to realise, too, that in Nepal and Sikkim the annual rainfall was sometimes as much as 200 inches, yet a few miles away in Tibet it averaged only twelve to fourteen inches a year. The monsoon clouds that make places like Kalimpong and Gangtok so fertile cannot pass over the great rampart of the Himalayas.

The food shortage and the climate tended to make the struggle between Tibet and China even more unequal. The Chinese were bringing in vast stores of winter clothes while the loss of their grazing grounds had robbed the Tibetans of even their sheepskins. The Chinese were well supplied with drugs against the murderous climate. The Tibetans had none. The best houses, the best land were by now Chinese possessions, inhabited and used by pure Chinese families imported to colonise their "backward" brothers.

Yet the Tibetans were still fighting against these incredible odds; and with all their paradoxes, with their filth (most Tibetans do not wash, the dirt being regarded as an extra protection against the cold), I found them a wonderful people, and it was impossible to live with them, however brief the encounter, without being immensely impressed.

One does not necessarily need to believe that the Dalai Lama, chosen in such an extraordinary fashion, is in fact a living Buddha. What it is important to realise is that millions of people (whose religion is probably as good as ours) do believe that to be the truth, and, despite the mumbo-jumbo that surrounds much of Buddhism, have achieved a real living faith, something they believe in so devoutly that it enters into their daily life to a depth and with a devoutness that many of us may well envy.

I know that when the time came for me to say farewell to my Tibetan friends I did so with a deep and genuine regret. I do not suppose I shall ever see them again. Many of them are possibly dead by now, for they were the ones who had fought from the first, the hard core of rebellion; and I am sure they were in at the death, when revolt came to Lhasa, and fighting spread to the streets of the capital to cover the escape of the God-king.

My mission was over and after the trek back I flew to London early in February. There were occasional reports from inside Tibet but they were very scanty until, little more than six weeks later, the bombshell burst. Heavy fighting had broken out in Lhasa. For a few days there was little more to add, but then, suddenly, the world was startled to learn that the Dalai Lama had escaped and was heading for India, hotly pursued by the Chinese.

The first news was conflicting and not until later did we really find out what happened in Lhasa in mid-March. So much of what I write now depends on a reconstruction of events based on talks which I and my friends, particularly

Heinrich Harrer, had with members of the Dalai Lama's party when he arrived at Tezpur.

When the first reports appeared of fighting in Lhasa and the first rumours of the Dalai Lama's escape filtered through, I was in Nyasaland, having flown there to study the political situation, but I immediately returned to the Himalayas which I had left so recently. It was one of the most wretched journeys I have ever made. I left Blantyre in Nyasaland on a Tuesday morning with a good connection at Salisbury in Southern Rhodesia for Nairobi, where I planned to pick up an east-bound plane, at 9.0 p.m., an hour after landing. Unfortunately the Salisbury–Nairobi aircraft was delayed for two hours with engine trouble. Everything depended on my catching the east-bound Constellation, so while I waited, I telephoned to London and pulled a few strings, with the result that Air India held up their plane at Nairobi for an hour—very considerate of them. I spent the night in the plane, reaching Bombay on Wednesday, where I had a shower, then took a twin-engined Dakota to a place called Nagpur, arriving there shortly before midnight on Wednesday. I waited at the airport for some hours for another small plane, which reached Calcutta at 6.0 a.m. At 8.0. a.m. I caught another aircraft to Bagdogra, reaching there at 10.30 a.m. on the Thursday. I shared a bus with several chickens for the ten-mile journey to Siliguri, then took the same old taxi over the winding hairpin bend to Kalimpong to meet my old friends and find out what was happening. I stayed there some time, then realised that Tezpur was the place to go to; so I returned down to Bagdogra, where I chartered a single-engined plane to Tezpur, the end of the line. What follows now is the result of those weeks I spent in India, flying backwards and forwards to the various places of interest.

X

ESCAPE FROM THE PALACE

It was the evening of March 17, 1959, in Lhasa. Night was falling over the city, but since mid-afternoon a sandstorm had already blotted out the daylight, and the Chinese garrison searchlights probed blindly into the dust that covered everything.

Around the Norbulingka, the summer palace of the Dalai Lama on the outer fringes of the city, a vast silent crowd of Tibetans huddled together, backs to the sand-laden blast, patiently keeping vigil. There were thousands of men, women and children, and they were there for one reason alone. They believed their leader was in peril from the Chinese. So they had come, volunteers all, to form an added rampart in front of the twelve-foot walls surrounding the palace.

But there was a stealthy movement by a gate in the north wall of the palace. Silently it was opened from the inside, and muffled figures slipped out and at once merged unseen into the darkness and dust. The gate closed behind them. Minutes later it opened again. A second and larger party emerged. There were court officials wearing their turquoise earring badges of office, there were mule drivers, soldiers and servants. And among them was a tallish spare figure wrapped in the faded sweatstained *chuba*, the all-enveloping maroon cloak of a servitor. This man's head was muffled in a rough knitted woollen cap pulled down well over his brow. His mouth and nostrils were covered against the sand as he turned his back on the walls of the palace and shuffled into the darkness with his companions. The Dalai Lama was on his way to freedom.

The immediate prologue to this drama in the dark had

taken place over several months, as larger areas of territory came under guerrilla control. All Chinese pretence of friendship and co-operation with the Tibetans had gone. The Chinese withdrew to their fortress strong-points, venturing out only rarely on punitive missions if they were in overwhelming strength. Day by day, week by week, the guerrillas moved nearer to Lhasa. They were growing in strength as well as daring. Their constant hit-and-run raids on Chinese outposts were winning them recruits from the countryside in an ever-increasing flow. Large bands were operating within a few miles of Lhasa itself.

Sitting in his headquarters at Lhasa, the Chinese military governor, General Tan Kuan-San, had reason to be alarmed. It was eight years since the armies of Mao Tse-tung had poured over the border from China and, far from being subdued, the normally peaceable Tibetans were growing more and more restive and resistant to the ideals of Marxist coexistence.

The key to it all, as General Tan realised, lay with the youthful Dalai Lama himself, for if he could be shown to his people as a true friend of the Chinese, things might quieten down, so the Chinese commander sent a flowery message to the God-king, the tenor of which was that the rebellious tribesmen were upsetting the work of the Communist new order, and it would be appreciated by Peking if His Holiness would show his sympathies with his Chinese comrades by putting his own personal bodyguard of 5,000 men into the fight against the rebels.

The Dalai Lama had no intention of being put in such a position and an equally flowery reply was sent to General Tan. Much as he regretted the constant bloodshed, which could never solve their problem, the Dalai Lama doubted the wisdom of using his bodyguard against their fellow-Tibetans for, as he pointed out, they were ill-trained and ill-equipped and would be no match for the ferocious Khambas.

General Tan tried again, offering to give the bodyguard new weapons and have them trained in modern warfare, but again the Dalai Lama found an excuse, replying that he felt he could not guarantee the bodyguard's loyalty to the Chinese, and that once in the field he feared they might desert to the rebels, taking over all the weapons so kindly provided.

This was a time of fascinating diplomatic thrust and parry, with the Dalai Lama showing himself to be more than a match for the Chinese as he played for time. These formal exchanges took many months, but Peking was growing impatient with General Tan's failure to obtain results, for the question of face was involved. Peking ordered Tan to tell the Dalai Lama that if he did not respond courteously when asked with courtesy, stronger measures might be necessary.

The next move was a formal invitation from Chou En-lai for the Dalai Lama to attend a meeting of the Chinese National Assembly in Peking in January.

The Dalai Lama countered by replying that much as he appreciated the honour, urgent religious affairs demanded his presence in Lhasa throughout |January. Chou En-lai offered to postpone the sitting of the Assembly to any date the God-king cared to mention, to which the Dalai Lama thanked him politely and said he would consider it, without committing himself in the least.

The Lhasa cabinet had no illusions about what would happen to their ruler if he were incautious enough to go to China. Some excuse would be found to placate world opinion, and the Dalai Lama would never be allowed to return to Tibet. Obviously, they argued, it must be made as difficult as possible for the Chinese to maintain contact with the palace. To hamper and forestall any further Peking moves they insisted that all approaches to the Dalai Lama must first be made through the cabinet, which would consider and advise.

For a few more weeks China grappled angrily with a mass of protocol and Tibetan red tape worthy of Whitehall at its worst. Then, failing completely to untangle it, early in March 1959 General Tan took a fateful decision. The Dalai Lama, he said, must visit him at his H.Q.—alone. Ostensibly the visit was to see a Chinese theatre performance. In fact, as was plain to the Dalai Lama, this was no social invitation. It was an order from the commander of the occupying forces and the order was expected to be obeyed.

General Tan thus revealed himself as one of the Far East's worst psychologists. If he had actually wanted to rouse public Tibetan feeling against him he could hardly have chosen more suitable means. To order the sacred Dalai Lama to attend as though he were a common mortal was a slap at the pride of every citizen of Lhasa. It was more. They took it as a calculated insult and reacted accordingly.

Students openly paraded the streets of Lhasa shouting anti-Chinese slogans, thousands of women marched to the Consulate-General of India imploring Nehru's help in presenting a protest petition to the governor. The monks in Lhasa's three great monasteries, seeing trouble ahead, lifted their flagstones and broke down false walls to reach their stores of hidden arms, kept against just such a moment as this. Some of the firearms they kept themselves. Others were passed quietly to the townspeople.

This was the sort of atmosphere in which rumours grew and sprouted like mushrooms in a meadow. Someone whispered that whatever the Dalai Lama replied to Tan he would be taken from his palace by force and spirited away to Peking. It spread like wildfire. On the morning of March 10 the women of Lhasa flocked to the gates of the Norbulingka palace. Organised by the wives of two high Tibetan officials, their numbers grew. Hourly more women, now joined by some men, picketed the great gates. They would not let the Chinese in. And, for his own safety, they were determined not to let their ruler out.

Heinig Harrer told of the next few hours, when writing for the *Daily Mail*:

"By noon (on March 10) the crowd, a dense throng of at least 10,000 men, women, and children, had surrounded all entrances to the Norbulingka. Its mood was angry. Giant banner slogans of 'Go Home, Chinese' were being carried. The crowd was aware that the Dalai Lama was due to attend the Chinese garrison theatrical performance one hour later. They were determined to prevent this.

"In the late afternoon the Dalai Lama sent the first of his now famous letters to General Tan.

"This stated, 'Dear Comrade Political Commissar Tan, I intended to go to the Military Area Command to see the theatrical performance yesterday, but I was unable to do so, owing to obstruction by people, ecclesiastical and secular, who were instigated by a few bad elements and who did not know the facts. This has put me to indescribable shame. I am greatly upset and worried and at a loss what to do'."

During the next few days the Dalai Lama maintained this correspondence with the governor.

Harrer's account continues:

"On March 16, the day before he fled, the Dalai Lama wrote:

"'A few days from now, when there are enough forces that I can trust, I shall make my way to the Military Area Command secretly. When that time comes I shall first send you a letter. I request you to adopt reliable measures. What are your views? Please write to me often.'"

Heinig interprets these letters as a ruse to hide from the Chinese any suspicion that he might be contemplating flight from Lhasa. If his theory is correct—and I am convinced it is—the ruse succeeded completely.

Meanwhile, the crowd outside the Norbulingka had swollen to 30,000. Chinese troops were confined to barracks but artillery posts were manned and heavy guns were trained on the Norbulingka and the Potala palaces. Tension mounted hourly, and finally, March 17, the Chinese field pieces opened fire.

It was not a barrage, just two shells which fell harmlessly in the Jewel Gardens surrounding the Norbulingka. Probably they were intended as no more than a warning to the crowd to disperse, or possibly the Chinese governor had become impatient at being confined to his quarters, unable to contact the Dalai Lama, helpless to break up the rebellious mob.

But whatever his reason, those two shells changed the course of Tibet's history. They convinced the Dalai Lama and his advisers that Tan really meant business. And the decision was taken. The God-king must flee from Lhasa secretly, without even his people knowing. That same night, under cover of the providential sandstorm, he slipped away.

Inside the Norbulingka everything went on as usual, and the efforts to cover the ruler's escape were so successful that even the Dalai Lama's personal photographer, a nobleman named Jigme Tering, though living in the next room to the commander of the ruler's bodyguard, did not know till three days later that he had gone.

For hour after hour after the Dalai Lama had left his palace the crowd remained on its self-imposed duty round the walls. There was no more shelling and the Chinese troops still remained in their quarters. Tibetans and occupiers alike had no suspicion that the God-king was already many miles away from Lhasa.

But the lull could not last, and on March 18 the Chinese commander sent a message to the summer palace requesting the Dalai Lama to leave, and guaranteeing him absolute safety. He also promised publicly that no harm would come to the citizens of Lhasa, "except for the upper strata reactionaries". The Chinese waited several hours for the answer which Oriental protocol demanded. To their astonishment there was no answer from the man they supposed still to be in the Norbulingka. The one certain fact is that never for a moment did the Chinese imagine that the Dalai Lama had already escaped.

When finally their message remained unanswered, the Chinese brought up more field guns and trained them on the Norbulingka from three sides. Early on the morning of March 19, they opened fire, with pauses to allow the Dalai Lama to escape. It seems clear they did not want to kill him, but only to make his palace untenable. By the end of the day the entire Norbulingka had been erased. Yet the vast crowd still ringed the ruined palace and its extensive gardens, still refusing to believe that the God-king was not somewhere inside. They stayed there on the night of the 19th, and only on the morning of March 20 did they learn the truth.

The news was the signal for a general uprising in Lhasa, led by units of the small regular Tibetan army and backed by both guerrillas, who had infiltrated into the city, and civilians.

The Lhasa garrison consisted only of six alternated regiments of Tibetan regular soldiers amounting to about 4,000 men. Against them were ranged the might of the Chinese forces, and they knew it must be a hopeless fight in Lhasa. The Chinese had 30,000 troops in Lhasa, and superior, more modern, arms. The Tibetans had only a few cannon which had to be wheeled into position by mules. They could not possibly match the modern Chinese guns, yet the Tibetans held the Chinese for five days. How many died will never be known. The reports of casualties vary from 5,000 to 15,000 Tibetans killed.

Most of the dead fell to relentless Chinese artillery fire. From batteries situated at commanding points round Lhasa the Chinese poured in a constant hail of shells. Special targets were the big university monasteries of Shera and Drepung, where more than 12,000 students and monks lived and prayed, but who now forsook their prayer wheels for arms and died in their thousands defending their monasteries.

As the Chinese fought the Tibetan troops, guerrillas started looting Chinese banks. The broadcasting station that poured out Peking's propaganda was sacked, and the mob then set on quisling noblemen who had sided with the Chinese, like sixty-eight-year-old Tsarong Shape, Tibet's richest man, who had long been the object of suspicion because his vast estates had never been touched by the Reds.

Tsarong rose to power in the Dalai's palace but for the past eight years had lived in his own ancient castle, in constant fear of a dagger thrust and guarded by rugged troops armed with rifles and knives. In the end they were of no avail and he was killed by the crowd.

Many of the Dalai Lama's bodyguard, who stayed to cover his retreat, were slaughtered. Two hundred of them were captured on the second day of the uprising, marched at the double in front of a Chinese machine-gun company and mown down to a man.

For two days the long-range artillery slaughter continued before the Chinese infantry appeared in the city in force. They found a smoking shambles. Houses were shattered, monasteries gutted, the streets littered with corpses. Mothers with children lay where they had fallen, a city of the dead. So heavy were the casualties that normal burial rites were out of the question. For when a Tibetan dies the most normal rite is for the dead to be cut up and cast outside the city to the vultures to eat the flesh and free the soul for its next incarnation. But this was impossible, so they turned to water, and thousands of bodies were flung into Lhasa's river to float away from the city.

But the savagery was by no means over yet. The rebels of Lhasa had been crushed. Now they had to be kept down. Chinese patrols searched from house to house. Where arms were found, whole families were shot on the spot. Thousands of monks were rounded up and driven away in army trucks to forced labour. Nuns were seized and put into Chinese Army brothels. Hundreds of people were flogged daily in public on suspicion of knowing the whereabouts of rebel survivors. Civilians wearing amulets with the portrait of the Dalai Lama were shot on sight. To mention the Dalai Lama's name meant arrest and—at the least—deportation to labour camps.

Fighting still goes on in many parts of Tibet. The Khambas are far from crushed. Lhasa has been martyred but it was no victory for the Chinese, for they were defeated—and they knew it—the moment the God-king slipped through their fingers.

XI

FLIGHT

The Dalai Lama was safely out of Lhasa, but now he had
a long, long way to go before he reached the real safety of
the Himalayan barrier that marked the frontier of Assam.

At first the high officials with him hoped he might be
able to trek towards Sikkim, and thence to Kalimpong
where the Dalai Lama had stayed before. The Lhasa–
Kalimpong route, which formerly took at least a month, if
not longer, can now be done in a matter of days by jeep;
but the very fact that it is one of the few jeep roads running
south to India means that the Chinese patrol it constantly,
and even the Khambas (so they told me earlier in the year)
had been unable to maintain sustained offensives in the area
of the road, for the Chinese had built permanent barracks,
and have check-points that are manned day and night. It
would have been as impossible for the Dalai Lama to pass
these check-posts as for anybody to pass a Customs post
linking two countries without the knowledge of the authorities.

In fact, while the one-sided battle was being fought
to its bitter end in the streets of Lhasa, the Dalai Lama
and his party safely crossed the Ramagang Ferry in an
ancient rectangular craft that could carry fifty people at
a time, then struck north for forty miles. This was not
only a ruse in the hope of outwitting the Chinese, it was
dictated by real necessity, for, with Lhasa virtually en-
circled, the southern exits were blocked. And, of course,
the "roads" are most primitive. The main road leading
south from Lhasa is through wild and rocky terrain with no
alternative "loops" or routes, and the road is frequently
so narrow that two yak teams cannot pass.

For forty miles the escaping party rode or walked north through the Pembu district, a country of violent scenery. They made a long traverse on a narrow ledge along the mountain range. At one time the party had to dismount, for, though mules or horses could negotiate the track, they could not possibly cross the deep ravines, linked by the same type of swinging chain bridges that I had had to use in Nepal. Actually, the terrain must have been very similar to that of Nepal and at roughly the same altitude of 14,000 to 16,000 feet.

Most of the Pembu district was in the hands of guerrillas, but not all, and though members of the party with whom I talked later were reticent about the narrow escapes during that first part of the journey, they made it quite clear that at one moment the whole party was very nearly caught by the Chinese.

This happened when the Dalai Lama, having gone forty miles north of Lhasa, walked twenty miles eastwards, then travelled south again with Lhasa perhaps about twenty miles to the west as he passed it. New mules had been furnished, but even though the party was all dressed in the rough robes of serfs, a caravan of ninety Tibetans would have caused immediate alarm if spotted by the Chinese. Their protection was pitifully small—certainly not more than sixty armed Khambas—and there was one highly dangerous spot that had to be crossed. This was the Lhasa–Chamdo road, built by the Chinese to link Lhasa with the east. To cross this road near Lhasa was highly dangerous, yet it was not possible for the party to travel farther east and cross it at a point farther away from Lhasa, for there was only one track leading north–south, and this crossed a gorge linked by a swinging bridge. It was therefore out of the question to make a diversion from the road (little more than a mountainous path anyway) and cross the main east–west road farther from Lhasa.

While the main party slept during the day just north of the vital road, Khamba scouts dressed as peasants tried to find a way across the road farther to the east. They re-

Tibetan women gathered outside the Potala palace in protest against the Chinese occupation of Tibet

The ferry on which the Dalai Lama escaped

The Dalai Lama (on the white horse) crossing the Zsagola pass in Southern Tibet on his flight to India

turned after several hours with the news that it was not possible. Even had the party been able to travel over trackless country, it would eventually have been stopped by sheer cliffs, hundreds of feet deep. No party could have descended the ravine, nor climbed the slopes on the other side, and there was no bridge across. There was only one thing for it—the east–west road had to be crossed at the one point where it was most likely to be guarded.

The party decided to cross by night after a day's rest in safe country. As at every resting place, the servants of the party made a dozen huts of bamboo for the nobles (I have seen Tibetans build these lean-to wattle or bamboo huts almost as quickly as a man can put up a tent). Twenty miles behind—that is north of—the party, Khambas guarded the rear. Westwards the fighting was raging in Tibet, and the Dalai Lama could even hear the guns of the Chinese as they systematically destroyed his summer palace and the Jewel Garden, believing him to be inside.

It was 10.0 p.m., probably on the night of March 20, when the party set off to cross the Chamdo road. The Chinese still had no inkling that the Dalai Lama had escaped. But as the scouts ahead of the main party reached the Chamdo road they found a small patrol of Chinese troops camped here, a dozen or so in all. They were not looking for the Dalai Lama; it was a purely routine patrol guarding what was in effect an important crossroads.

The scouts returned to the main party about midnight, stopping the Dalai Lama less than an hour's march from the road. The party dismounted and made tea while twenty Khambas moved silently southwards towards the road. The engagement was sharp and decisive. The Khamba officers had tommy-guns and so had all the Chinese. The Khambas crept up on the unsuspecting patrol and attacked, using the knife. Five Khambas were killed instantly from machine-gun fire. Eight Chinese were killed, but unfortunately three escaped—northwards.

It was a small battle, as battles go, but it was extremely important. The three escapees were never caught, but within

H

a few hours Peking was broadcasting—long before any-body else—that the Dalai Lama had been abducted by brigands.

We shall never know for certain what happened, but it is probable that one or more of the escaping Chinese soldiers fled north up the very road down which the Dalai Lama was travelling. The Dalai Lama had camped by the side of the track in a small valley with a stream of good water, and probably the Chinese escapees discovered the camp, and though they would not recognise the Dalai Lama in his serf's clothes, the size of the party must have indicated its importance. They probably got the word through to the Chinese commander in Lhasa, only a few miles away, that same night. Whatever happened, a few hours after the Dalai Lama had crossed the Chamdo road, just before dawn, three of the Khambas covering his rear caught up with the escape party and warned the Dalai Lama that the Chinese knew he had escaped. There was no more question of secrecy. A hurried conference was held at first light. The Dalai Lama was still so near to Lhasa, and moving southwards, that the Chinese naturally assumed he was making for Sikkim. And it was at this dawn conference, in yet another hastily-constructed bamboo hut, that the Khambas decided on one last great gamble to outwit the Chinese by forming a decoy group to put them off the scent.

But it could not be done too soon, for as yet the Chinese did not know exactly where the Dalai Lama was, and with the Chamdo road behind him, the Dalai Lama was moving into country where Tibetan guerrillas controlled much of the area. So the party moved southwards—with Chinese troops very close behind—until they reached a spot just north of Lake Yamdrok.

Just after dusk, north of the lake, the party of ninety halted. The servants set about making huts for the night and the Dalai Lama, still in serf's clothing, held a council of the men in the party, consulting the oracles and the three cabinet ministers who were travelling with him. The

Master of Tea supervised the brewing of Tibet's favourite beverage, and when the tea had been passed round, the decision was made for the party to split into two.

By the light of the small camp-fires, volunteers were asked for from the Khamba ranks. Every single man without hesitation offered to lay down his life for the God-king, and in the end thirty were chosen by ballot. One of the nobles who was there said later, when he arrived at Tezpur, that those who drew the "lucky" sentences of death reacted with the greatest joy, while there was no consoling those unlucky enough to be omitted from the suicide squad. It is certain now that the heroism of the thirty Khamba guerrillas who formed this squad saved the life of the Dalai Lama as Chinese troops chased him towards the border, for these men lured the Chinese off the trail while the Dalai Lama headed eastwards, and deliberately leaked false news that they were escorting the Dalai Lama towards Nepal.

The ruse was just in time, for when the Chinese learned the Dalai Lama had escaped, believing him certain to take the Sikkim road, they moved twelve lorries of troops up to the town of Thangia, farther south than the Dalai Lama's party, with the object of cutting the road. Some informants say that the Khambas were told of this by a series of runners. Others swear that the Khambas in this region had radios and flashed the news northwards.

What does seem certain is that the party halted for a day at Lake Yamdrok. Then the decoy group moved off in the direction of Gyangste, stopping at the first village to let the false news leak out that they were escorting the Dalai Lama to Sikkim. The entire community came out to see the man they thought was the Dalai Lama. Some reports say that the Khambas kept one member of their party dressed in russet robes half hidden as though pretending this was the Dalai Lama himself. Within a few hours of leaving the main party, the decoy group had passed through several villages. At each one they deliberately let it be known that they were escorting the Dalai Lama, swearing the villagers to secrecy, knowing perfectly well that, either through a quisling or carelessness, the Chinese would surely find out what was happening. This ruse was certainly the reason why the first reports of the Dalai Lama's escape indicated that he was moving towards Sikkim. And it would appear likely that the early stories of an injury to the Dalai Lama when his horse fell on a mountain track were probably put out by the decoy group of Khambas as well.

Within a matter of hours the Chinese knew—or thought they knew—exactly where the Dalai Lama was. The Khamba party was deliberately moving slowly as it approached the main road leading from Lhasa to Sikkim, and the only jeep road in the area.

Down this the Chinese hastily despatched enough reinforcements to deal with the situation. They were absolutely confident they would catch the Dalai Lama, and orders were given that he was to be taken alive. With the road cut farther south (by the twelve lorries of troops at Thangia) the Chinese now sent six truckloads of troops southwards from their garrison at Gyangtse, and when the trucks could no longer operate they set off eastwards on foot to meet the advancing party.

To the Chinese success must have been utterly sure. Both to the north and the south the Dalai Lama was cut off. The Chinese thrust eastwards from the main road over the mountains leading to Lake Yamdrok, and the decoy group moved westwards along the same wild and almost impassable tracks. They met two days later close to the 15,000-foot Karo Pass, and the result of the battle was never in doubt. The Tibetans were outnumbered four to one, the Chinese were all equipped with tommy-guns. Since every single Khamba was apparently killed, the details will never be known, but it seems that the fighting continued for several hours, partly because the Tibetans were using the mountain slopes for cover in an engagement that consisted at first largely of sniping, and partly because the Chinese were terrified of an indiscriminate attack that might result in the death of the Dalai Lama. In the end, I suppose, the Chinese must have discovered they had been tricked, but by then the Dalai Lama was so far ahead on tracks unsuitable for motorised traffic that the Chinese had no chance of catching him up before he crossed into Assam. He was also by then in the heart of Khamba-held country. As George Patterson says (*The Daily Telegraph*, April 15, 1959):

"From Lhokha, south of Lhasa, to Tsona Dzong, the point of exit on the Tibetan–Assam border, the Dalai Lama passed through guerrilla-held country where they are in complete control of 55 dzongs or districts, covering an area of roughly 10,000 square miles, and number a supposed 25,000 troops. Not only could the Chinese not follow him into this territory when they knew he was heading south, but it will take them a long time, perhaps several years if the guerrillas' ammunition and supplies hold out, to clear this area of high mountains, narrow trails and precipitous valleys."

From now on, the journey was less eventful. It had become, in fact, one hard slog, but at least from the time the party left Lake Yamdrok it was able to travel by day, and without too much haste, eastward across the Bumla range of Himalayas, and then southward to the frontier. It took fifteen days for the party, which had left Lhasa on March 17, to reach the frontier.

India meanwhile had alerted various check-points along the frontier north of Bhutan and the North-East Frontier area, though the Indian authorities had no contact with the Dalai Lama or his party. The Indians' first real concrete information about the Dalai Lama's whereabouts came when an emissary of the Dalai Lama showed up at an Indian check-post at Chutamghu during the afternoon of March 29. The officer there could not send the information to the divisional headquarters (which was a two-day mule-ride away) by radio. So an official of Chutamghu rode to the sub-divisional headquarters with the information. From there it was transmitted to another station and finally it reached Shillong on March 31 at 8 p.m. The Government of India received information of the Dalai Lama's entry on April 1.

It is interesting to note that when the Dalai Lama's emissary, carrying his request for sanctuary in India in his turquoise-studded dagger and scabbard, delivered it to India's check-post at Chutamghu, it was written in the Dalai Lama's own hand in broken English on thick parchment paper and bore his personal seal. This means that he brought out his seals of office, which the Chinese were at first reported to have seized.

When, on the evening of March 31, the Dalai Lama crossed the check-post, he had with him a party of eight, including his mother, a sister, and his younger brother. The retinue of seventy-two arrived later.

To the Lok Sabha (the Indian Parliament) Nehru made the following announcement on April 3:

"The other day, three days ago, I think, when speaking about recent happenings in Tibet, I mentioned that I would keep the House informed about further development. In the last two days, i.e., the day before yesterday and yesterday, we have been receiving a number of messages. They have to go through a rather devious route.

"Yesterday I was thinking of informing the House of a certain development, but then I hesitated to do so as I wanted to fully confirm it and was also waiting for some details. We received them last evening. But I thought I should inform the House first."

Nehru added: "The facts are that on April 1, day before yesterday morning, we received a message from Shillong, dated March 31 evening, that an emissary with a message from the Dalai Lama had arrived on our border check-post, Chutamghu, in NEFA. (North-East Frontier Agency.)

"The emissary had arrived there on March 29 stating that the Dalai Lama had requested political asylum and that he (Dalai Lama) was expected to reach the border on March 30.

"We received the message on April 1, the same evening a message was received by us again from Shillong, dated

April 1, that the Dalai Lama with a small party of eight had crossed into our territory on the evening of March 31.

"We had expected some such development might occur and we had instructed the check-posts what to do in case such a development took place. So, when he crossed over into our territory, the Dalai Lama was received by our assistant political officer of the Tawang sub-division, which is part of the Kamang Frontier Division of NEFA. A little later, the rest of his party came in. The total number, who have come with him or after him, is eighty.

"On April 2 we learnt that his party, in two groups, is moving towards Tawang, and that the Dalai Lama is expected to reach Tawang on Sunday, April 5."

So, as I waited at Tezpur, ended the first stage of this great journey. Nehru had said the party numbered eighty, but in fact it was about ninety, and by the time it crossed into Indian territory it included a senior tutor, a junior tutor, three cabinet ministers, the Lord Chamberlain, three Lord Attendants (the Master of Ceremonies, the Master of Robes, the Master of Tea); the Dalai Lama's mother, sister and brother; a chamberlain, a secretary general, an incarnate Lama of Draye, one representative of Sera monastery, and a representative of Drepong monastery, together with officials and servants.

On April 5, as Nehru had prophesied, the God-king and his party reached India's greatest Buddhist monastery, Tawang, 10,000 feet high in the heart of the prohibited North-East Frontier Agency.

XII

ARRIVAL IN INDIA

Although it had taken place only a few months previously, my march across the Himalayas to meet the guerrillas already seemed to belong to the remote past. So much had happened so quickly, it was almost forgotten. But as soon as I arrive at Tezpur, and as the Dalai Lama crossed into Indian territory, I set about making plans to climb up into the mountains to meet him.

George Patterson was already in Tezpur, and I also met there a new friend, John Osman of *The Daily Telegraph*, a most likeable and hardworking youngster with whom I shared a bedroom for some time. We decided to pool our resources and try to trek up to Bomdila in defiance of regulations imposed by the Indians but which we did not feel justified in accepting as fair in view of India's attitude to Tibet.

Unfortunately, we were completely unsuccessful. I knew that, after Tawang, the Dalai Lama would have to pass by Bomdila, a pass at 10,000 feet and recently linked by a new jeep road to the plains of Assam. But this road was denied to us, as were all roads in the prohibited NEFA, and so we tried to persuade guides to take us up to Bomdila through the jungle paths. We very nearly pulled it off. I bought my equipment (such as it was) in Tezpur, though I could not buy a tent. We bought blankets, haversacks, thick walking-sticks, a large supply of food. I felt the walk to Bomdila by "back tracks" would take perhaps five days (though it could be done in a day by jeep) and though I was worried about having no tent at 10,000 feet, I decided to chance it. For some days I reconnoitred the ground. The mountains started about thirty miles north of Tezpur and the plains in front of them were largely composed of tea gardens.

Osman and I chartered a light aircraft to study the lie of the land, and, with the help of local friends, we soon found a way across through a tea plantation. The journey would have to be made by night in elephant country, but we had no alternative. Eventually we set off for a point half a mile from the frontier of NEFA, laden with supplies. There we were to meet our guides who had already been interviewed and who had agreed to accompany us on payment of a large sum of money. But when we arrived late at night they deserted us, and without guides it was quite impossible to go on. The area was filled with troops, the tracks (apart from the main Bomdila road) were almost invisible, the country was alive with tiger and elephant. We would have been lost within a few hours of starting our excursion.

When the guides became frightened, I even offered them in desperation the princely sum of a thousand rupees each as a bonus, but their fear of the Assamese troops was stronger than their avarice. There was nothing left but to return to Tezpur.

Osman and I were able to fly over the area, past Bomdila and up in the Tawang district which the Dalai Lama reached on April 5. From the single-engined plane I could see why the Dalai Lama and his party could move at no more than fifteen miles a day.

As we twisted and turned round the mountains we could see only narrow sandy tracks like thin pencil lines in the thick jungle. The difficulty was obviously that, walking against the grain of the Himalayas, the Dalai Lama's journey was not along the mountains, but up and down and across them.

Sometimes he would climb for two days and then descend for two days. Most of his journey was on horseback, and his trip was not made easier by the reports of enemy agents harassing his route, though these reports were never confirmed.

Of all the moving moments in the Dalai Lama's journey—
even including the arrival at Tezpur—none matched the
scene when he reached Tawang, the greatest Buddhist
monastery in India, gleaming white on a grassy spur,
10,000 feet above sea-level, and surrounded by dense, unexplored forests where no plane could land. In a magical
ceremony lit by a thousand Buddhist butter-lamps and with
the devout lining the route for ten miles before he reached the
monastery, the Dalai Lama entered the great library of
Tawang monastery, which houses 700 priceless Tibetan
books each two feet long, and sat at a specially-made throne
for ceremonial Buddhist dances before going to pray in the
central great temple in front of an image of the Lord
Buddha in gold.

How like a dream Tawang must have looked to the tired
traveller! For 350 years the monastery at Tawang has
stood atop its mountain with its colony of Buddhist monks.
From time to time it has been hit by earthquake, and the
ancient walls of the building stand in need of repair, but
they had been freshly whitewashed and, as the Dalai Lama
approached with his caravan, monks advanced to meet him,
starting fires with sprigs of juniper to drive away evil
spirits. That first night chairs were arranged in the great
library, and on his makeshift throne the Dalai Lama sat for
two hours during the ceremonial dances. Then he went to
the chapel, which is decorated with gold leaf, and prayed
before the butter-lamps ranged along an altar flanked by
giant Buddhas.

Tawang, though so remote, has a population of about
30,000 and over half massed in the ragged streets to greet
the Dalai Lama. For hours his entourage was unable to
pass the hillsides that lead to the monastery, for thousands of
people had slept the night in the cold to await his coming,
hundreds of them a day's march or more out of Tawang.
For mile after mile along the narrow tracks, sometimes only
a yard wide and with precipitous drops, men and women
lined the route.

Lamas with enormous trumpets, some of them twelve

feet long, had congregated at regular intervals along the route. At one point a tent made of flowers was put up in case the Dalai Lama wanted to rest. Tibetan tea was ready for him. He stopped and sipped a little tea served in silver cups, relics of the mother of the sixth Dalai Lama, and brought out of the great temple for the occasion.

The first thing the Dalai Lama did when he passed through the monastery gates was to wash and lie down for an hour alone in one of the monastery's hundreds of cell-like rooms used for sleeping and meditation. Then, after ceremonial tea, he came out. The courtyard was jammed with thousands of people and the scene must have been incredibly beautiful and colourful as the Dalai Lama distributed to the people the balance of the provisions he had brought into India.

He escaped from Lhasa with more than two months' supplies, and men, women and children—shouting, "Hail, Dalai Lama, thrice blessed be the Holy One"—scrambled for the food.

After dusk the local Monpa tribe erected an open-air stage with wooden boxes and bamboos and put on the biggest theatrical show ever seen at Tawang.

The Monpas love the theatre and have an extensive wardrobe of costumes and masks and a large repertory— usually called dances, but actually dramatic performances embodying warriors, animals, and birds. The most impressive were the Thutoldam actors who, dressed realistically as skeletons, portrayed the experience of the soul after death. The performances went on for hours.

The Monpas, who were playing their part as India's hosts to the Dalai Lama, are gentle, friendly, courteous and industrious. They love music and have a passion for bright things decorated with mitre-shaped hats, silver swords and daggers. They live in good, cosy, double-storeyed houses. The women are pretty with wheat-complexioned, oval faces, high cheekbones and raven hair tied in plaits.

But even before the Dalai Lama reached Tawang, the

little town of Tezpur had been turned topsy-turvy by the horde of journalists and photographers which was swiftly congregating there to await him.

I was lucky in arriving early, and when I flew in by charter plane with John Osman our pilot arranged for a jeep to take us to the secretary of the Tezpur Station Club where there was thought to be some sleeping accommodation. The secretary was away, so the driver took us to the nearest bungalow to the airfield—and who should be lolling on the balcony in pyjamas but that cheerful bearded missionary George Patterson.

The occupants of the bungalow, Ronald and Mary de la Rue Browne, were out, but George said it would be all right and we dumped our bags and a boy brought us large jugs of orangeade. When the Brownes returned they took the invasion without the flicker of an eyelid and insisted that we stay with them until the Dalai Lama's arrival. They were most generous and made us more than welcome in their bungalow, twelve miles out of Tezpur and set amid the delicate green tea gardens that make Assam so beautiful.

My first task was to find a car and hire it by the week, and even this took some doing in Tezpur, and the only one I could get was so ancient that water had to be poured into the radiator every five miles, while the horn, so necessary in India, needed the application of a screwdriver each time after use. It was driven by a boy whose name sounded like Sawdust, so Sawdust he became, and on the first day his car broke down for an hour on a jungle track because of water contamination in the local petrol. After an hour's trek through the jungle—an exercise not to be dismissed lightly— I found a bicycle rickshaw, but the Indian had only just started light-heartedly to peddle me off for help to the nearest garage seven miles away when his saddle fell off. This was followed by a puncture. I returned to the car at which moment an elephant carrying a load of wood passed by. The elephant boy offered to pull my car into town.

There were no hotels in Tezpur for the hundred or so

correspondents who were gathering there. The Tezpur Station Club had two beds, but for most of the time there was no running water, and it had no cooking facilities. In a lean-to shack behind the main club building was a store which sold tinned goods, and for a consideration it was sometimes possible to persuade the billiard marker to heat them up, if he was not busy keeping score. The club was a white and black building with snooker every evening and tennis on Tuesdays and Fridays. There was a long bar with local beer at seven shillings a pint, a price which did not seem to prohibit a steady sale.

Here we all awaited the Dalai Lama's arrival in a town which once was known as the garden city of Assam, its dusty streets criss-crossed, like paths edging the sea, between artificial lakes that were fed from the waters of the Brahmaputra. It needed much skill to keep these lakes filled, for the Brahmaputra is a womanly river, constantly giving birth to new sandbanks that change its course, as the pilots of the flat-bottomed river steamers know only too well. But as in the past it was the working centre of a large Assam tea-growing district, there were many willing hands to organise the labour required to keep Tezpur looking pretty if not clean. The sheets of water cooled the town on hot days and, when the dawn sun chased away the fierce night rains, there were mornings when the lakes steamed with the heat so that as you walked the streets it was like walking through narrow lanes cut into banks of fog.

One lake even lapped against the white walls of a British bank where the tea planters used to draw that small portion of their earnings they did not put into savings back home in Britain. The bank had now gone, with most things British, and in its place was the severely correct and hopelessly inefficient State Bank of India, its symbol a bedraggled man at the front entrance with a shotgun across his knees. By the bank the lake had dried into a vast pit, perhaps five acres in all, scarred, overgrown with weeds, like a bomb site, with a film of water in the centre in which a few grey water buffalo tried in vain to escape the heat.

The streets were filled with refuse piled up in front of each squalid shop, and on the edge of the town, ten miles past the bamboo trees that lined the rutted road, was an airport, once a flourishing base for flying men and materials "over the hump" to the Chinese Nationalists, but now closed except briefly when the planes came in from Calcutta. The wandering perimeter was overgrown and potholes a foot deep frightened even the local Indian jeep drivers. In front of thatched huts, peasants laid out their chillies to dry like crimson carpets nestling under the lee of the old concrete bomb-loading bays. It was like a ghost town, the old airport; like the opening sequence of a film about past glories that starts with a scene of ruin then takes the picture-goer back to the people who inhabited it before ruin overtook them. It did not need much imagination, as I jeeped along the worn concrete, to see again the aircraft nosing down, youth pulling off its collective flying helmet, and making a dash for the mess and a pint of beer.

But then the whole of Tezpur was a kind of ghost town evoking memories of an era now dead and gone, and what place could be more ironically fitting than this dirty run-down township as the stage for the last act in the drama of the Dalai Lama's escape from Tibet?

Here the Press of the world waited for the day of arrival while a succession of minor Indian officials made it increasingly clear that India would do everything possible to prevent any real contact with the Dalai Lama, and that Nehru thoroughly disapproved of what was going on.

The man selected to travel to Bomdila to meet the Dalai Lama was a Tibetan-speaking Indian called Mr. P. N. Menon, a little too stout and a little too smooth, but who had once held a position in Lhasa. It was quite obvious that Mr. Menon was going to seize this opportunity of getting his photograph and name into the papers on every conceivable occasion, an effort in which he thoroughly succeeded, largely by stolidly remaining in every foreground, even on the Dalai Lama's throne at

Tezpur, during the celebrations. Later Menon became the janitor of the Dalai Lama's "prison" at Mussoorie.

But then I can never reflect on official India's attitude to Tibet without my gorge rising. I must say that the irony of the situation—in which Nehru was finally *forced* to sympathise with the Tibetans—appealed to me, for, though it is not my purpose here to engage in a slanging match, I honestly believe Pandit Nehru's special brand of two-faced politics has done an incalculable amount of harm to the world's attempts to attain peace; but nothing has ever been so smoothly wicked as his handling of Tibet. I had many talks about this with Heinrich Harrer. Heinig and I became good friends, and long after the Dalai Lama had arrived, he and I lunched together in London on the very day in which he wrote some of his thoughts on this subject in the *Daily Mail* (May 15, 1959):

"It is clear to all close observers that Nehru is determined to isolate the Dalai Lama from his advisers and persuade him to return without them to Lhasa. As Nehru sees it this would be a tidy and convenient solution for India to the whole Tibetan problem. The Dalai Lama would have to become a Chinese puppet, but the Chinese would stop saying nasty things about the Indians.

"And that is all Nehru wants. Like Pilate, he wishes to wash his hands of the whole embarrassing affair as quickly as possible. Tibet's tragedy is that she knows it is useless to take her case to the United Nations, but because of Nehru's cynicism she cannot get from India as much help as even little Austria gave to Hungary.

"Nehru says that the Chinese have a right to rule Tibet. He smugly says it is high time social reforms were introduced in this backward land.

"But who is he to talk, and what knowledgeable man would call Chinese Communism a social improvement on Tibetan feudalisms? Is this not a classic case of the man in the glass house throwing stones?

"What are the facts? Nehru runs a nation which contains

millions of undernourished, starving, illiterate, poverty-stricken and often roofless people. Peking is busy establishing throughout China a commune system which represents nothing less than the complete enslavement of 650,000,000 people.

"The monks and noblemen of Lhasa, through the Dalai Lama, ran a feudal State with the kind of laws you had in England in Tudor Times. But were your Tudor ancestors any less happy than you are today? No one starved in Tibet until the Chinese came. There was always an abundance of food. Tibet has no Calcutta where human poverty and degradation reach their lowest ebb.

"Nehru, who talks glibly about the need for social reforms in Tibet, runs a city where humans die in the streets of starvation. That could never have happened in free Tibet."

How right was Heinig. And now suddenly Nehru, whose vacillating policy over Tibet had astonished not only the world but finally India itself, faced a serious political decision over the future of Tibet. Remembering that the Dalai Lama, on his way down to Bomdila, was not only a Living Buddha but Tibet's political leader, Nehru could no longer dismiss, as he had done, what was happening in Tibet as "a clash of wills" between Tibet and China. In fact, the fighting in Tibet provided one half of a remarkable phenomenon, that of two, not one, great religions of the world fighting the menace of Communism—the Buddhists in the East and Islam (ironically largely in the form of Nasser) in the Middle East.

Though there was no connection between the two it did mean that these two great religions had joined with Christianity in damning for ever the scourge of Communism. But until the Dalai Lama's escape, Nehru, who can be more than volatile when he attacks the British Commonwealth, had maintained a restrained if undignified silence on what was happening. Nasser's *volte face* (which may in the long run have a profound influence on the side of democracy)

Tibetans laying down their arms to Chinese troops after the fighting in Lhasa

Fallen telegraph poles and tangled wire littering a street in Lhasa after the fighting

Monks of the austere yellow sect praying for the safety of the Dalai Lama

The Dalai Lama (seated middle front) with his Khamba warrior guard

Nehru dismissed by saying how "grieved" he was that Egypt and Russia, both friends of India, were having a quarrel; and as for Tibet, he still referred to it as "the Tibet region" of China.

Why did Nehru adopt this incredibly timid attitude, especially in view of his sharp criticism of Britain over Suez in which he did not hesitate to say what he thought of us? Why so frightened over a problem that was so much nearer his own frontiers? There are three possible reasons. The first is that Nehru, despite the many critics in his own government, has for long attached far greater importance to his relations with the eastern Communist *bloc* than to his relations with the Commonwealth. The second is that Nehru has for an equally long time been frankly frightened of the Chinese and the Russians and has not dared to say what he has, I hope, privately thought. The third conclusion I drew was actually a mixture of the two former reasons: that Nehru has been, and is, both afraid and drawn to the Communist *bloc*.

This was all very well while the Tibetan revolt was being hushed up deliberately by Nehru, but now things were different. Not only had it become quite clear that China's aggression in Tibet was naked and against all her promises to the Dalai Lama, but the evidence was mounting that the Chinese in Tibet were consolidating their positions all along India's northern frontier. With the Dalai Lama given sanctuary in India, Nehru had in fact given political asylum to the leader of a nation—and the leader of a religion—to which he had previously given the unpalatable advice that it should adopt a policy of non-violence against their Chinese masters. By giving refuge to the Dalai Lama, he would soon be faced with the prospect of giving sanctuary to thousands of Tibetan refugees. What would he say to them, these people whose only desire in life was to be left outside the rest of the troubled world?

It was very interesting to note that on April 8, when I was in Tezpur, Nehru was forced quietly to rescind an order virtually banning all male Tibetan refugees. Though only a

I

few days previously most male Tibetan refugees were being told to return to Tibet when they reached the border, a high-ranking officer suddenly announced that officers were now quietly permitting them to enter on direct instructions from Nehru. The change of policy was kept very quiet.

This change, which Nehru did not like at all, was undoubtedly forced on him when he realised that the conscience of India itself had been aroused over Tibet in much the same way as the conscience of the West was aroused over the rape of Hungary. Leading Indian statesmen were bitterly criticising their leader since the news of the fighting had grown grimmer. In fact this was Nehru's Budapest. It was true, of course, that he could no more go to war for Tibet than the West could have gone to war for Budapest. But these days we live in a world where, odd though it may seem, words do frequently count as much as deeds and where the pen is often mightier than the sword.

The Russian aggression in Hungary did more harm to the Communist cause, and made more people loathe the Russian leaders, than anything since the war. It was a setback from which they have never recovered, a political setback. They still have Hungary under their heel but the voice of the world condemned them in such a fashion that they will never in the eyes of the world live down their shame, and even though the cynical Soviet leaders may laugh it off at their Kremlin parties one cannot overestimate what it really means in the long pages of history. Who can tell, for instance, what effect Hungary had on the thinking of Islam?

During the Hungarian fighting, Nehru kept a timid silence but now with Tibet on his doorstep would he dare to do the same again? For the inescapable fact is that the Chinese dissolution of the Dalai Lama's Government meant in effect the tearing up of the Sino–Tibetan Treaty of 1951 recognising Tibet as an autonomous region under China. If this were so, surely it means that the 1954 Sino–Indian Treaty on Tibet (based as it was on the aforementioned treaty) was also no longer valid? How, in view of the past few weeks, could Nehru maintain his official attitude that "nothing really important is happening in Tibet"? It would be easy to dip a pen in vitriol and launch a vicious attack on Nehru, for he has certainly made many unfair and bitter attacks on Britain and the Commonwealth, but this is not the time, and it would perhaps be unfair, for Nehru is, I believe, a tortured man who dare not combine his public and private emotions. But now on his own frontiers the wind of freedom was dying down and the storms of force and tyranny were howling around his very ears, and Nehru was finding at last that he not only had to face the voices of an outraged world which he affected to ignore, but the even stronger voices of his own countrymen, bitterly disillusioned, and which could one day be strong enough even to topple him from his ivory tower.

All this was happening as Mr. Menon was jeeping up to Bomdila and the Dalai Lama was walking down from Tawang. Again I tried to penetrate NEFA, again without success. I then motored to a town called Guhati, and chartered another plane with John Osman, and together we set off to fly to Bomdila, and, if possible, beyond. There was no possibility of landing in this almost unexplored area, but I wanted to see the Dalai Lama's party on the trail and if possible photograph it. The country was very much the same as that I had traversed with Izzard (our party number-ing nearly fifty) and it would have been very easy to spot them.

Unfortunately we chose a day when the weather in the mountains suddenly worsened. We pin-pointed Bomdila, but when we tried to follow the only track leading north-wards to Tawang, we repeatedly lost it in thick cloud. Towards nightfall we had to give it up and landed at a small township called Jalpaiguri, spending the night in the Jalpaiguri Club, an ancient run-down building with Osman and myself the only two people in it, and eating a coarse supper in a room marked "dining-room".

On April 8 the Dalai Lama left Tawang on the first

stage of the sixty-two mile march to Bomdila, a journey of four to five days. On the first day he reached a village called Jang, then had to negotiate a very difficult stretch of mountainous territory leading up to the 14,500-foot Se-La. ("La" means "pass".) The journey took him through 17,000-foot ranges topped by three peaks under snow. After that it was fairly easy going to the 10,000-foot pass at Bomdila which he reached on April 12, and where Mr. Menon was awaiting him ready to instruct the Dalai Lama on how the Indians expected this embarrassing visitor to behave.

The Dalai Lama was expected to stay at Bomdila until the morning of April 17, but right until the last moment there was some doubt, for the heavy pre-monsoon rains had almost washed away the jeep track from Bomdila to Foot-hills, the village at the frontier of NEFA, and where the Assam plains start, thirty miles from Tezpur.

Fortunately on April 16 the rains eased up, and early in the morning of April 17—a Friday—the Dalai Lama got into a jeep station-wagon and set off on the 10,000-foot descent to the plains. On that Friday night, just a month since the Dalai Lama escaped from Lhasa, the God-king of all Buddhism spent his last night in the mountains, resting beneath a bamboo and thatch hut erected before his arrival at Khaleng, ready to jeep down the last ten miles on the Saturday to a good road, a good car, good food, and a fantastic multitude of worshippers that were awaiting him in the tiny "tea-town" that had suddenly sprung to life as the drama of the Dalai Lama's escape gathered momentum.

At Tezpur, bamboo barriers were being erected to control the crowds, a couple of shacks had been knocked down because they were in the way, and even the drains were being cleaned out.

Waiting for the Dalai Lama was his brother—under armed guard because he was a Chiang Kai-shek man—and his last favourite premier, the venerable Lukhwangha who escaped from Tibet in 1956, and who was living in a small

boarding-house in Tezpur, an imposing figure in his blue
robes.

That last night at Khaleng it rained very heavily again,
but the Dalai Lama blessed the people of the tiny village
before he retired. The next morning he was up before
dawn, ready to drive ten miles to meet an inquisitive world.

XIII

COMMENT BY THE DALAI LAMA

Now that I come to end this volume, so many months after the day when I stood in Tezpur watching the Dalai Lama's magnificent arrival, two predominant thoughts are still uppermost in my mind; both make me realise how impossible it has been to approach my task with impartiality. The first thought concerns China, the second India.

I have long believed that Asia's particular brand of Communism, as practised by Red China, is in many more ways more dangerous than the Communism of Soviet Russia. I certainly believe that the seeds of any future war are being sown in Asia rather than in Europe; and I see no reason to hide my loathing at the Chinese rape of Tibet; a disgraceful case of wanton aggression against a quiet, peace-loving nation, made with the sole object of exterminating it—and I use the word exterminating advisedly, for that is exactly what the Chinese are doing in Tibet at present.

Neither do I see any point in masking my disgust at the hypocrisy of Pandit Nehru, a man who must bear a large share of the responsibility for what is happening in Tibet today. Given a little courage, Nehru might have been enormously influential in helping Tibet to reach a compromise with Red China. But Nehru is spending his ageing years preaching the glories of freedom while paying lip service to the forces dedicated to the suppression of all that liberty stands for.

How true were the Lord Buddha's words, "Rely on yourselves, do not rely on external help." Buddha was talking about the salvation of the soul, but as the Dalai Lama arrived in India, which virtually imprisoned him behind barbed wire, those words, uttered six centuries before the birth of Christ, were ominously applicable to the world at large and to India in particular.

On the other hand, both these sordid aspects of world politics may benefit mankind in the end. For the first time in my many visits to India I found on this occasion a deep stirring of conscience amongst intelligent Indians, combined with a genuine embarrassment at the rôle played by their Government; and this feeling may well awaken India to a more serious sense of responsibility to the free world. I hope so. I have always loved India, and count many Indians amongst my close friends, and nothing would give me greater pleasure than to see this great country and its mystical people cross the narrow bridge that divides politics from statesmanship. The Chinese, too, may well rue the day the Dalai Lama escaped, for the Dalai Lama's flight made quite different impressions on the West and the East.

To us of the West, much of the fascination of the Dalai Lama's escape story lay in the hardship of the journey and the way in which the Chinese were outwitted; that and the political significance of what was happening. To the people of Asia the journey was taken as casually as we would take an Atlantic crossing; as a journey it was not to them very remarkable; nor were they very much interested in the political aspect, since to them this was merely another incident in the age-old skirmishing between China and Tibet.

To Asia the most shocking aspect of the affair was the religious one; and just as Russia did herself incalculable harm over the rape of Hungary, so the Chinese have lost enormous face in the eyes of their fellow Asians not over the rape of Tibet, but over the persecution of a Living God. Imagine what would happen if our God were among us again and was then chased from one mountain top to another by anti-religious savages. It would start a world war. The effect of the Dalai Lama's escape, and the way the Chinese hounded him, was just as profound on the peoples of Asia. The people of Asia are intensely religious, and they have the ability, often denied to the people of the West, of genuinely respecting the gods of religions in which they may not believe, so that Hindus in India felt as indignant and outraged about what was happening in Tibet as the Bhuddists themselves. This was by far the most important reason for Indian public opinion forcing a frightened Nehru to come out with expressions, however tame, of sympathy for the Tibetans. It certainly influenced thinking Indians far more than the military threat to their northern borders.

Above all, India could not ignore the statement which the Dalai Lama made at Tezpur and its devastating condemnation of Red China.

Here it is as it was read out in English on the lawn of the Circuit House on that hot Saturday morning.

"It has always been accepted that the Tibetan people are different from the Han people of China. There has always been a strong desire for independence on the part of the Tibetan people. Throughout history, this has been asserted on numerous occasions. Sometimes, the Chinese Government have imposed their suzerainty on Tibet, and at other times, Tibet has functioned as an independent country. In any event, at all times, even when the suzerainty of China was imposed, Tibet remained autonomous in control of its internal affairs.

"In 1951, under pressure of the Chinese Government, a seventeen-point agreement was made between China and Tibet. In that agreement, the suzerainty of China was accepted as there was no alternative left to the Tibetans. But even in the agreement it was stated that Tibet would enjoy full autonomy. Though the control of External Affairs and Defence were to be in the hands of the Chinese Government, it was agreed that there would be no interference by the Chinese Government with the Tibetan religion and customs and her internal administration. In fact, after the occupation of Tibet by the Chinese Armies, the Tibetan Government did not enjoy any measure of autonomy even in internal matters, and the Chinese Government exercised full powers in Tibet's affairs. In 1956, a Preparatory Committee was set up for Tibet with the Dalai

Lama as Chairman, the Panchen Lama as Vice-Chairman and General Chang Kue-hua as the Representative of the Chinese Government. In practice, even this body had little power and decisions in all important matters were taken by the Chinese authorities. The Dalai Lama and his Government tried their best to adhere to the seventeen-point agreement, but the interference of the Chinese authorities persisted.

"By the end of 1955 a struggle had started in the Kham Province and this assumed serious proportions in 1956. In the consequential struggle, the Chinese Armed Forces destroyed a large number of monasteries. Many Lamas were killed and a large number of monks and officials were taken and employed on the construction of roads in China, and the interference in the exercise of religious freedom increased.

"The relations of Tibetans with China became openly strained from the early part of February 1959. The Dalai Lama had agreed a month in advance to attend a cultural show in the Chinese Headquarters and the date was suddenly fixed for the 10th of March. The people of Lhasa became apprehensive that some harm might be done to the Dalai Lama and as a result about ten thousand people gathered round the Dalai Lama's summer palace, Norbulingka, and physically prevented the Dalai Lama from attending the function. Thereafter, the people themselves decided to raise a bodyguard for the protection of the Dalai Lama. Large crowds of Tibetans went about the streets of Lhasa demonstrating against Chinese authority. In spite of this demonstration from the people, the Dalai Lama and his Government endeavoured to maintain friendly relations with the Chinese representatives as to how best to bring about peace in Tibet and assuage the people's anxiety. While these negotiations were being carried out, reinforcements arrived to strengthen the Chinese garrisons in Lhasa and Tibet. On the 17th March, two or three mortar shells were fired in the direction of the Norbulingka palace. Fortunately, the shells fell in a near-by pond. After this, the advisers became alive to the danger to the person of the Dalai Lama and in those difficult circumstances it became imperative for the Dalai Lama, the members of his family and his high officials to leave Lhasa. The Dalai Lama would like to state categorically that he left Lhasa and Tibet and came to India of his own free will and not under duress.

"It was due to the loyalty and affectionate support of his people that the Dalai Lama was able to find his way through a route which is quite arduous. The route which the Dalai Lama took involved crossing the Kyichu and the Tsangpo rivers and making his way through the Lhokha area, Yarlung valley and Tsona Dzong before reaching the Indian Frontier at Kanzey Mane near Chuthangmu.

"On the 29th March, 1959, the Dalai Lama sent two emissaries across the Indo–Tibetan border requesting the Government of India's permission to enter India and seek asylum there. The Dalai Lama is extremely grateful to the people and Government of India for their spontaneous and generous welcome as well as the asylum granted to him and his followers. India and Tibet have religious, cultural and trade links extending over a thousand years and for Tibetans it has always been the land of enlightenment, having given birth to Lord Buddha. The Dalai Lama is deeply touched by the kind greetings extended to him on his safe arrival in India by the Prime Minister, Shri Jawaharlal Nehru, and his colleagues in the Government of India. The Dalai Lama has already sent reply to this message of greetings.

"Ever since the Dalai Lama entered India at Kanzey Mane near Chuthangmu, he has experienced in full measure the respect and hospitality extended to him by the people of the Kameng Frontier Division of the North-East Frontier Agency and the Dalai Lama would like to state how the Government of India's officers posted there had spared no efforts in making his stay and journey through this extremely well-administered part of India as comfortable as possible.

"The Dalai Lama will now be proceeding to Mussoorie which he hoped to reach in the next few days. The Dalai Lama will give thought to his future plans and, if necessary, give expression to them as soon as he has had a chance to rest and reflect on recent events. His country and people have passed through an extremely difficult period and all that the Dalai Lama wishes to say at the moment is to express his sincere regrets at the tragedy which has overtaken Tibet and to fervently hope that these troubles would be over soon without any more bloodshed.

"As the Dalai Lama and the spiritual head of all the Buddhists in Tibet, his foremost concern is the well-being of his people and in ensuring the perpetual flourishing of his sacred religion and freedom of his country.

"While expressing once again thankfulness at his safe arrival in India, the Dalai Lama would like to take this opportunity to communicate to all his friends, well-wishers and devotees in India and abroad his sincere gratitude for the many messages of sympathies and concern with which they have flooded him."

This statement was issued by the Dalai Lama on April 18, 1959, shortly before he entrained for Mussoorie. He was followed by a hundred journalists who expected to be afforded facilities to see the Dalai Lama if the Dalai Lama so wished—and it was quite obvious that he did wish this, but Nehru absolutely refused to allow the Press to see the Dalai Lama until two months later—on June 20.

Why? For one simple reason. Nehru knew full well that the international reporters from cities as far away as New York and London could not possibly afford the time to hang on, and he knew that when they had gone, the resident reporters in India (who can be expelled summarily if Nehru dislikes what they write) would be the only ones left. The general clamour would have died down, and the conference would by then have far less sensational coverage in the international Press, and so embarrass India less in her relations with Communist China. Nehru went to inordinate lengths to stop reporters seeing the Dalai Lama. Among those who followed him to Mussoorie was Heinrich Harrer and a *Daily Mail* reporter, Rhona Churchill, who had this to say in the *Daily Mail*.

"The Dalai Lama, his mother, his sister, his young

brother, and his Ministers are today caged up in a small enclosure on the top of a hill outside Mussoorie.

"They are entirely surrounded by a 14-ft.-high barbed-wire fence which looks painfully reminiscent of the outer wall of a German concentration camp.

"They are allowed no communication with the outside world.

"The Dalai Lama's mother personally at Tezpur asked Heinrich Harrer to call on her as soon as she reached Mussoorie, saying: 'Then I can tell you all about our experience.'

"Since she entered the shabby villa that is now her home Harrer has not been allowed to see her.

"Surkhang Lhacham Kusho, the attractive wife of the senior lay Cabinet Minister, went out of her way to seek him out the morning she arrived within the barbed-wire compound and asked him to call on her husband and herself later to 'have a long talk'.

"I was standing close by as they chatted together like old friends when suddenly an Indian security guard in plain clothes brusquely separated them without even a polite word of explanation.

"It was quite obvious to me after watching the behaviour of these senior Tibetans that they were all anxious to have a chance as soon as possible to tell their old friend Heinig the full story of their recent experiences both in Tibet and during their flight.

"It was equally obvious that the Indian Government has gone out of its way to prevent them from so doing or, in fact, from speaking to any member of the Press. Not only are they prisoners here, but they also have no freedom of speech.

"Several members of our Press corps have witnessed these various incidents, yet when I asked Mr. P. N. Menon, the Dalai Lama's camp commandant, for an explanation he blandly said none of them had occurred.

"When I told him that the Dalai Lama's mother had invited Mr. Harrer to visit her, he said: 'That cannot be true for she has not mentioned such an invitation to me.'

"I asked: 'Am I to understand from that that the Dalai Lama's mother is not free to invite Mr. Harrer or anyone else to her new home without first asking your permission?'

"Mr. Menon, who has been actually sleeping and living in the same house as the Dalai Lama and his family and acting as his guard dog, said: 'You can understand what you like.'"

Eventually, on June 20, the Dalai Lama was permitted to hold a Press conference. He preceded the conference with this statement:

"Ever since my arrival in India I have been receiving almost every day sad and distressing news of the suffering and inhuman treatment of my people. I have heard almost daily with a heavy heart of the increasing agony and affliction, their harassment and persecution and of the terrible deportation and execution of innocent men. These have made me realise forcibly that the time has manifestly arrived when in the interests of my people and religion and to save them from the danger of near annihilation, I must not keep silent any longer but must frankly and plainly tell the world the truth about Tibet and appeal to the conscience of all peace-loving and civilised nations.

"To understand and appreciate the significance and implication of the recent tragic happenings in Tibet, it is necessary to refer to the main events which have occurred in the country since 1950.

"It is recognised by every independent observer that Tibet had virtually been independent by enjoying and exercising all rights of sovereignty whether internal or external. This has also been implicitly admitted by the Communist Government of China, for the very structure, terms and conditions of the so-called agreement of 1951 conclusively show that it was an agreement between two independent and sovereign States. It follows, therefore, that when the Chinese armies violated the territorial integrity of Tibet they were committing a flagrant act of aggression. The agreement which followed the invasion of Tibet was also thrust upon its people and Government by the threat of arms. It was never accepted by them of their own free will. The consent of the Government was secured under duress and at the point of the bayonet.

"My representatives were compelled to sign the agreement under threat of further military operations against Tibet by the invading armies of China leading to utter ravage and ruin of the country. Even the Tibetan seal which was affixed to the agreement was not the seal of my representatives but a seal copied and fabricated by the Chinese authorities in Peking and kept in their possession ever since.

"While I and my Government did not voluntarily accept the agreement we were obliged to acquiesce in it and decided to abide by the terms and conditions in order to save my people and country from the danger of total destruction. It was, however, clear from the very beginning that the Chinese had no intentions of carrying out the agreement.

"Although they had solemnly undertaken to maintain my status and power as the Dalai Lama, they did not lose any opportunity to undermine my authority and sow dissensions among my people. In fact, they compelled me, situated as I was, to dismiss my Prime Ministers under threat of their execution without trial, because they had in all honesty and sincerity resisted the unjustified usurpations of power by representatives of the Chinese Government in Tibet.

"Far from carrying out the agreement they began deliberately to pursue a course of policy which was diametrically opposed to the terms and conditions which they had themselves laid down. Thus commenced a reign of terror which finds few parallels in the history of Tibet. Forced labour and compulsory exactions, a systematic persecution of the people, plunder and confiscation of property belonging to individuals and monasteries and execution of certain leading men in Tibet, these are the glorious achievements of the Chinese rule in Tibet.

"During all this time, patiently and sincerely I endeavoured to appease my people and to calm down their feelings and at the same time tried my best to persuade the Chinese authorities in Lhasa to adopt a policy of conciliation and friendliness. In spite of repeated failures I persisted in this policy till the last day when it became impossible for me to render any useful service to my people by remaining in Tibet. It is in these circumstances that I was obliged to leave my country in order to save it from further danger and disaster.

"I wish to make it clear that I have made these assertions against the Chinese officials in Tibet in the full knowledge of their gravity because I know them to be true. Perhaps the Peking Government are not fully aware of the facts of the situation.

"But if they are not prepared to accept these statements let them agree to an investigation on the point by an international commission. On our part I and my Government will readily agree to abide by the verdict of such an impartial body.

"It is necessary for me to add that before I visited India in 1956 it had become increasingly clear to me that my policy of amity and tolerance had totally failed to create any impression on the representatives of the Chinese Government in Tibet.

"Indeed they had frustrated every measure adopted by me to remove the bitter resentment felt by my people and to bring about a peaceful atmosphere in the country for the purpose of carrying out the necessary reforms. As I was unable to do anything for the benefit of my people I had practically made up my mind when I came to India not to return to Tibet until there was a manifest change in the attitude of the Chinese authorities. I therefore sought the advice of the Prime Minister of India who has always shown me unfailing kindness and consideration. After his talk with the Chinese Prime Minister and on the strength of the assurances given by him on behalf of China, Mr. Nehru advised me to change my decision.

"I followed his advice and returned to Tibet in the hope that conditions would change substantially for the better and I have no doubt that my hopes would have been realised if the Chinese authorities had on their part carried out the assurances which the Chinese Prime Minister had given to the Prime Minister of India.

"It was, however, painfully clear soon after my return that the representatives of the Chinese Government had no intention to adhere to their promises. The natural and inevitable result was that the situation steadily grew worse until it became impossible to control the spontaneous upsurge of my people against the tyranny and oppression of the Chinese authorities.

"At this point I wish to emphasise that I and my Government have never been opposed to the reforms which are necessary in the social, economic and political systems prevailing in Tibet.

"We have no desire to disguise the fact that ours is an ancient society and that we must introduce immediate changes in the interests of the people of Tibet. In fact, during the last nine years several reforms were proposed by me and my Government but every time these measures were strenuously opposed by the Chinese in spite of popular demand for them, with the result that nothing was done for the betterment of the social and economic conditions of the people.

"In particular it was my earnest desire that the system of land tenure should be radically changed without further delay and the large landed estates acquired by the State on payment of compensation for distribution amongst the tillers of the soil. But the Chinese authorities deliberately put every obstacle in the way of carrying out this just and reasonable reform. I desire to lay stress on the fact that we, as firm believers in Buddhism, welcome change and progress consistently with the genius of our people and the rich tradition of our country.

"But the people of Tibet will stoutly resist any victimisation, sacrilege and plunder in the name of reforms—a policy which is now being enforced by the representatives of the Chinese Government in Lhasa.

"I have attempted to present a clear and unvarnished picture of the situation in Tibet. I have endeavoured to tell the entire civilised world the real truth about Tibet, the truth which must ultimately prevail, however strong the forces of evil may appear to be today. I also wish to declare that we, Buddhists, firmly and steadfastly believe in peace and desire to live in peace with all the peoples and countries of the world. Although recent actions and policies of the Chinese authorities in Tibet have created strong feelings of bitterness and resentment against the Government of China, we Tibetans, lay and monk alike, do not cherish any feelings of enmity and hatred against the great Chinese people.

"We wish to live in peace and ask for peace and goodwill from all the countries of the world. I and my Government are, therefore, fully prepared to welcome a peaceful and amicable solution of the present tragic problem, provided that such a solution guarantees the preservation of the rights and powers which Tibet has enjoyed and exercised without any interference prior to 1950.

"We must also insist on the creation of a favourable climate by the immediate adoption of the essential measures as a condition precedent to negotiations for a peaceful settlement. We ask for peace and for a peaceful settlement but we must also ask for the maintenance of the status and the rights of our State and people.

"To you, gentlemen of the Press, I and my people owe a great debt of gratitude for all that you have done to assist us in our struggle for survival and freedom. Your sympathy and support has given us courage and strengthened our determination. I confidently hope that you will continue to lend that weight of your influence to the cause of peace and freedom for which the people of Tibet are fighting today."

At the conclusion of the statement, the Dalai Lama answered the following questions put to him by the Press:

Q: Your Holiness, from the reports you have been getting from Tibet, what are the Chinese Communists up to?

A: The ultimate Chinese aim with regard to Tibet, as far as I

K

can make out, seems to attempt the extermination of religion and culture and even the absorption of the Tibetan race.

Q: How?

A: Besides the civilian and military personnel already in Tibet five million Chinese settlers have arrived in eastern and north-eastern Tso, in addition to which four million Chinese settlers are planned to be sent to U and Sung provinces of Central Tibet. Many Tibetans have been deported to China, thereby resulting in the complete absorption of these Tibetans as a race, which is being undertaken by the Chinese.

I will give you a brief statement on recent events as reported to me by my people.

The people of Lhasa (the capital), both men and women, have been classed into three groups. The first group is deported to China where its fate is not known. The second group is imprisoned, interrogated and punished without limit in various Chinese military headquarters in Lhasa. The third group is fed with the meanest food and driven to forced labour. Each is made to carry 100 loads of earth daily, failing which, no food is given.

Armed troops are posted in the streets of Lhasa, where no more than two Tibetans are permitted to converse and where only aged men and women are to be seen. The central cathedral and other places of worship are closed. In addition, the reserves of the Tibetan Government and the properties of private individuals are being listed by the Chinese, who are conducting an all-out propaganda for the formation of people's communes.

Q: An Indian report filed with the International Commission of Jurists says that 65,000 Tibetans have been killed in fighting with Chinese occupation forces since 1956. Is this correct?

A: The number of Tibetans killed in fighting the Chinese occupation forces since 1956 is actually more than the Indian report.

Q: Is it true, as this report says, that a "deliberate and precise campaign has been conducted by the Chinese in Tibet against the Buddhist religion"?

A: The report is correct in stating that, until 1958, over 1,000 monasteries were destroyed, countless Lamas and monks killed and imprisoned, and the extermination of religious activity attempted. From 1955 onward a full-scale campaign was attempted in the provinces of U and Sung for the full-scale extermination of religion. We have documentary proof of these actions, and also of actions against the Buddha himself, who had been named as a reactionary element.

Q: Are younger people being indoctrinated in Communism?

A: Yes, it is true that the younger generation of Tibetans is being indoctrinated and the policy of colonisation is being practised.

Q: What made you finally decide to leave Lhasa?

A: On March 17, 1959, at 4 p.m., two mortar shells were fired towards my residence, as evidence of the Chinese intention to use military force, and, although I had endeavoured to keep up friendly relations with them for the last nine years, my hopes of rendering any service in the interests of my people by remaining in Tibet were finally shattered. Therefore, I and my Government had to leave for India secretly at 10 p.m. on March 17, 1959, with a view to rendering more beneficial service to my people.

Q: Did the Chinese attempt to block your escape?

A: The Chinese had no idea of my escape or else they would have certainly tried to intercept. They would not have succeeded in capturing me because of the unity of purpose of the people and the national voluntary defence army of Tibet.

Q: Is the revolt still going on in Tibet? Is any part of the country under the control of the Khambas?

A: As Tibet is a large country, there are still some parts where fighting is going on. However, there are several places to the east and north of Lhasa which are under the control of the Khambas.

Q: Would passive resistance by your people have gotten better results than an armed uprising?

A: Until the last day, I tried to bring about a peaceful settlement, the failure of which resulted in the armed uprising of my people who were compelled to fight for their freedom.

Q: Is it true that there are now Russian troops in Tibet, along with the technicians already known to be there?

A: I have heard such a report but I have no clear information yet as to how far it is true.

Q: Recently you wrote three letters to the Chinese authorities in Tibet. What had you hoped to accomplish?

A: I wrote the three letters to the Chinese at a critical time when the lives and bodies of innumerable people were in the hands of the Chinese. This was a measure adopted in order to take peaceful action. When the circumstances in which these letters were written were brought to the attention of the world they could not have made any other impression than to expose the measure of Chinese oppression.

Q: What do you think of the Preparatory Committee for Tibetan Autonomy which the Chinese have set up, with the Panchen Lama as acting chairman?

A: The Preparatory Committee for Tibetan Autonomy is nothing but nominal, with all powers concentrated in the hands of the Chinese. The Panchen Lama has no alternative but to carry out the orders of the Chinese. He has no actual power.

Q: Is there any agreement between you and the Panchen Lama as to what is best for Tibet?

A: The Panchen Lama has been under Chinese influence ever since his boyhood and has never enjoyed any freedom.

Q: Do you consider the 1951 treaty between Tibet and the Chinese Government still in force?

A: The Sino-Tibetan Treaty imposed by the Chinese in accordance with their own desires has been violated by the Chinese themselves, thus giving rise to a contradiction. Therefore we cannot abide by this agreement.

Q: Could you define the "autonomy of Tibet" that was supposed to be guaranteed by that agreement?

A: The autonomy of Tibet is meant to be the right of self-government in internal affairs, but the existing situation in Tibet gives no rights whatever to my Government.

Q: How much support is there for the present Government in Lhasa?

A: The present Government in Lhasa is nothing but a deceptive Government with all the power in the hands of the Chinese. The people of Tibet will never recognise it.

Q: Do Tibetans still recognise you and your ministers here with you as the Government of Tibet?

A: Wherever I am, accompanied by my Government, the Tibetan people recognise us as the Government of Tibet.

Q: Have any Communist Chinese diplomats talked to you about Tibetan affairs since you fled Lhasa?

A: No.

Q : Do you expect India's support in solving your problems?

A : I hope the Government of India will give us the same support, if not more, as she has given to small countries like Algeria, Morocco or Tunisia.

Q : Is India placing any restraints on your movements, as the Communists claim?

A : The Government of India has not placed any restraint at all on my movements, and if the occasion arises I intend to tour India and abroad.

Q : Do you plan an international appeal—for example, to the United Nations?

A : In case I am not satisfied by the terms of peaceful settlement offered by China, then I shall consider my future plans.

Q : Will you appeal for arms on behalf of the rebels?

A : Although I have no intention of keeping the national volunteer defence army unaided, I am intending to help them by means of peaceful solutions rather than military force.

Q : Under what conditions would you return to Lhasa?

A : I will return to Lhasa when I obtain the rights and powers which Tibet enjoyed and exercised prior to 1950.

Much has happened since the Dalai Lama started his flight from Lhasa, and though there seemed to be nothing the world could do about the unhappy plight of Tibet, in the month of that perilous journey across the mountains and its fearsome chain bridges, the adventure became one that enthralled the world. Day by day it grew in drama until the whole world—the whole free world that is—waited in suspense for the day when the Dalai Lama would finally reach the safety and comfort of the Assam plains.

Finally that day arrived but, as I say, there seemed little the world could do about it except sympathise. Yet that sympathy is not to be dismissed too lightly, however cold the comfort may seem for the Tibetans themselves. For there is nothing the free world can do at the moment about Tibet; not yet. Even so, world emotions cannot be denied for ever. These are the tides that shake the foundations of empires built on greed and lust and cruelty; no emperor ever born has been powerful enough to stand against them for ever, and though for the moment Tibet is "forgotten" and the world knows little of what is happening, Tibet is not dead, nor is the "Tibetan question", in the conscience of the world.

This may all sound very pompous to ardent Tibetologists, disillusioned with the world's complete inability to help small nations in distress; it is not meant to be pompous; I find it rather hard to say to people with whom I have become so close and so friendly and whom I admire so greatly, "Don't think too badly about the rest of the world—there's nothing we can do at the moment but hang on, the day of reckoning will come."

I only hope it will not come too late; on the other hand it is gratifying to think that the Chinese Communists, who from a distance appear so all-powerful, can in fact make such fools of themselves as to chase a God-king whose name is holy throughout half the world. It was as crass an error as Soviet Russia's mistake in Budapest; a classic example of overplaying the hand.

It is on this note that I would end this book; a note of hope, not of despair. A great deal has happened since I first set off from Katmandu on that long march across the Himalayas, there to pierce for the first time the secret that surrounded the war the world knew nothing about; a war behind barriers of this strange and mystic land that was to lead in a matter of weeks to the flight of the Dalai Lama himself, and to plunge me once more into this exciting drama and to be eyewitness to its climax.

It seems such a long time since Tobgye Wangdue came striding into our camp, in his sheepskin, and to the nights when Ralph Izzard and myself sat round the camp-fires listening to history until then secret; then the journey back, Africa, then that madcap flight across half the world from the slaughter of Africans in Nyasaland to the fighting in Tibet; the long wait in the bungalow of that kind-hearted couple, the de la rue Brownes, and finally the last broiling Saturday in Tezpur, and the final moment of that day when the ancient locomotive chuffed out of Tezpur's station carrying the Dalai Lama to Mussoorie. Heinig Harrer and I were on the station to wave him on his journey, and I am not ashamed to say there was a lump in my throat as I stood on the platform. With that same wonderful serene smile the Dalai Lama, behind the carriage window, put his palms together in front of his chest—the Tibetan's hail or farewell—and then he was lost to view as he set off in his air-conditioned coach to a new life, the life of an exile driven from his home, but the life of a man of stature and courage, and the life, I most devoutly hope, of a man not only with a past but with a future.

CHRONOLOGY OF EVENTS

August 1947. India becomes independent and the Government of India assumes existing treaty rights, including extra-territorial rights, and obligations of the United Kingdom in regard to Tibet, and the British Mission in Lhasa becomes the Indian Mission.

November 1948–January 1949. Nationalist armies collapse in north and central China; the Communists take Peking.

December 21, 1948. The Chinese Communists establish a North China People's Republic.

September 21, 1949. Chinese People's Political Consultative Conference convenes in Peking.

October 1, 1949. The People's Republic of China is inaugurated.

November 24, 1949. Radio Peking announces that the Panchen Lama (age thirteen) had appealed to Mao Tse-tung to "liberate" Tibet.

January 1, 1950. "Liberation" of Tibet is announced by the Chinese People's Government as one of the main tasks of the "People's Liberation Army".

August 5, 1950. New China Agency quotes General Liu Po-chen, Chairman of the South-west China Military Affairs Commission, as stating that Tibet must be brought back to the "Motherland's big family" and China's defence line must be consolidated.

August 1950. Tibetan delegation arrives in New Delhi for negotiations with the Chinese People's Representative.

August 24, 1950. Indian Ambassador in Peking informally points out to the Chinese Government the desirability of settling the Tibetan question peacefully; the Chinese reply that they regard Tibet as an integral part of China, but have no intention of forcing the issue and are willing to negotiate with Tibetan spokesmen for a settlement.

September 1950. Chinese Communist ambassador arrives in New Delhi and talks begin between the Tibetan Mission and the Chinese Embassy; the Chinese emphasise that talks cannot be held with a mission on foreign soil and desire transfer of talks to Peking, to which the Tibetan representatives agree.

September 30, 1950. Chinese Premier Chou En-lai, on first anniversary of the People's Republic of China, declares that Tibet "must be liberated".

October 7, 1950. Chinese forces invade Tibet.

October 19, 1950. Chamdo is captured and Tibetan defences crumble.

October 24, 1950. Radio Peking announces that Chinese forces had been ordered to advance into Tibet "to free three million Tibetans from imperialist oppression and to consolidate the national defences of China's western frontier".

October 25, 1950. Tibetan delegation in India leaves New Delhi for negotiations in Peking.

October 26, 1950. India sends a Note to the People's Republic protesting against the use of force against Tibet and stating that the invasion was not in the interests of China or of peace.

October 30, 1950. The Chinese Government replies to Indian Note stating that Tibet is an integral part of China, that the problem of Tibet is entirely a domestic problem, that the people of Tibet must be liberated and that "no foreign interference shall be tolerated in the problems of Tibet". It also states that the departure of the delegation to Peking was intentionally delayed under "outside instigation".

October 31, 1950. Indian Government sends a second Note making it clear that India has no political or territorial ambitions in Tibet and does not seek any new or privileged position, but protests that the use of force "could not possibly be reconciled with a peaceful settlement". Possibility of outside instigation categorically denied.

November 7, 1950. Tibet protests to the United Nations against the invasion and charges open aggression.

November 15, 1950. El Salvador files a request for a debate on Tibet in the General Assembly of the United Nations but on November 24 the matter is postponed *sine die* by the Assembly.

November 17, 1950. Dalai Lama is formally installed by Tibetans.

December 1950. Dalai Lama leaves Lhasa and sets up temporary government at Yatung, near the Indian border.

May 23, 1951. Peking announces the signing of the Seventeen-Point Agreement Treaty.

April 29, 1954. India signs agreement with China renouncing extra-territorial rights in Tibet, agreement to the "five principles of peaceful coexistence".

September 16, 1954. Dalai Lama arrives in Peking to attend the National People's Congress and remains for a six-month stay.

March 12, 1955. Peking announces that a Committee has been named for the preparation of "regional autonomy" for Tibet.

October 1, 1955. Preparatory Committee for the Autonomous Region of Tibet is inaugurated.

May 2, 1956. Rumours of political unrest in Tibet are spread at the coronation of the King of Nepal.

May 17, 1956. Reports from India confirm that the Chinese garrison in the Golak district of North-east Tibet was attacked by the Mimang monastic sect (also called Tibetan People's Committee).

July 17, 1956. Reports are received of the movement of heavy tanks into Tibet.

August 7, 1956. Liu Ke-ping, Chairman of the Nationality Affairs Committee of the National Congress, states that there had been a rebellion in western Szechwan but denies reports that there is any revolt in Tibet proper or that there are any religious or nationalistic overtones to the rebellion.

September 20, 1956. Nepal and China sign a treaty in which Nepal recognises China's sovereignty over Tibet and surrenders the concessions it possessed in Tibet under the treaty of 1856.

November 15, 1956. Reports reach India concerning new fighting between Tibetan rebels and Chinese forces.

November 25, 1956. Dalai Lama and Panchen Lama arrive in New Delhi to take part in observance of twenty-fifth centenary of the death of Buddha.

December 10, 1956. Chou En-lai, on a visit to India, admits report concerning armed conflict between Chinese troops and a "group of people" in Szechwan but states that it is over; assures Mr. Nehru that Tibet would enjoy autonomy and that China would not force Communism on Tibet.

December 19, 1956. Reports reach Nepal that Chinese Communist planes have bombed the Tibetan village of Kham Chiri Gawa.

February 27, 1957. Mao Tse-tung, in his speech on "Contradictions", announces that Tibet is not ready for the introduction of Communist reforms during the Second Five-Year Plan (1958–62).

March 1957. At a session of China's People's Political Consultative Conference (C.P.P.C.C.), a Tibetan representative, Po-pa-la, reports that unrest is still rife in Tibet, while another Tibetan representative reports that the uprising in Szechwan was among the Tibetan peoples of the area.

March 25, 1957. Radio Peking announces that Nepalese troops have been withdrawn from Tibet on March 18.

April 1, 1957. Dalai Lama returns to Lhasa from India.

April 22, 1957. The decision to postpone social reforms in Tibet until after 1962 is formalised in a government decree; speakers at a rally in Lhasa marking the first anniversary of the formation of the Preparatory Committee for the Autonomous Region of Tibet refer to continued unrest in Tibet and General Chang Kuo-hua, Commander of the Chinese army units in Tibet, appeals for "constant vigilance against the subversive activities of imperialist elements and the rebellious activities of separatists".

June 16, 1957. Radio Peking announces plan to withdraw Chinese Communist cadres from Tibet.

August 1, 1957. The *Tibet Daily* (Lhasa), in an article by Tan Kuansan, political commissar of the Chinese Communist army stationed in Tibet, declares that escapees from Tibet are carrying out subversive activities in Tibet and threatens a counter-blow by People's Liberation Army in accordance with the Seventeen-Point Treaty on the peaceful liberation of Tibet.

August 23, 1959. The *Tibet Daily* reports that an "armed rebellion" is still in progress in the eastern part of Tibet.

February 9, 1958. Reports are made at the meeting of the Nationality Affairs Commission of the State Council concerning continuing unrest in Tibet.

March 9, 1958. New China News Agency (Peking) announces the reorganisation of the Preparatory Committee for the Autonomous Region of Tibet by increasing the representation of the Tibetans.

July 27, 1958. Prime Minister Nehru of India cancels his proposed visit to Tibet in September 1958 at the suggestion of the Communist Chinese Government.

August 1, 1958. Reports reaching India state that a full-scale revolt is in progress in Tibet.

October 1, 1958. Tsinghai *Red and Expert* political journal comments on armed uprising and counter-revolutionary activity in Tsinghai bordering Tibet.

November–December, 1958. Reports continue on unrest in Lappa Island in Tibet as well as in areas neighbouring China.

January 1, 1959. Panchen Lama promises in New Year's message to Mao Tse-tung to work for the suppression of sabotage in Tibet.

March 9, 1959. Dalai Lama is invited for a cultural programme on the next day, 1 p.m., and asked to come unaccompanied by any of his ministers or bodyguard.

March 10, 1959. Crowds gather around the palace and are

assured by the Dalai Lama that he will not attend the cultural programme.

March 11, 1959. A meeting of governmental officials is called at the palace and a proclamation is issued in the name of the cabinet declaring that Tibet is independent.

March 12, 1959. A meeting is called at Shol, below the Potala palace, concerning the declaration of independence and action necessary for its implementation.

March 12–17, 1959. Meeting at Shol in continuous session.

March 17, 1959. Chinese troops fire two shells on the palace.

March 17, 1959. Dalai Lama leaves palace for escape to India.

March 19, 1959. Serious bombardment begins at 1 a.m., with Norbulingka palace as a target; Tibetans launch attacks against Chinese garrisons.

March 23, 1959. Concern is expressed by Mr. Nehru about the safety of the Dalai Lama.

March 28, 1959. Peking reports that the rebellion has been crushed by March 22, that some 20,000 rebels were involved, that the Tibetan Local Government has been dissolved and that the Preparatory Committee for the proposed Tibetan Autonomous Region shall exercise the functions and powers of the Tibet Local Government.

March 31, 1959. The Dalai Lama and his party reach India and are granted political asylum.

April 7, 1959. New China News Agency reports "some armed rebels" still active in Tibet and that the Panchen Lama appeals to the new Government of Tibet for its help in "thoroughly suppressing" them.

April 8, 1959. Tibetan rebels proclaim a provisional Government.

April 9, 1959. Indian Defence Minister Mr. V. K. Menon states that Indians would defend their country "if anybody should be unkind and transgress our territory".

April 10, 1959. The Panchen Lama, on his way to Peking to attend the 2nd National People's Congress, states that he firmly believes the rebellion will be thoroughly crushed.

April 18, 1959. The Dalai Lama arrives in Tezpur, India, and a statement is issued.

April 20, 1959. Prime Minister Nehru declares that the Dalai Lama will be free to pursue religious activities but not to indulge in politics.

April 24, 1959. Mr. Nehru confers with the Dalai Lama at Mussoorie.

April 27, 1959. Mr. Nehru refutes allegations made by "responsible persons" in Peking that India was used as a base by the rebels, that the Indians have actively aided them, and repeats his invitation to the Panchen Lama or any other Peking emissary to visit the Dalai Lama.

April 29, 1959. The Panchen Lama at the 2nd National People's Congress in Peking criticises "certain political circles in India for unfriendliness" and rejects Mr. Nehru's invitation to visit India as "unnecessary . . . The Tibetan question can only be solved in Tibet".

April 30, 1959. The Panchen Lama states that the rebellion in Tibet has been, on the whole, liquidated, that order has been re-established and that "democratic" reforms are being actively implemented.

June 6, 1959. The Dalai Lama grants interview to Mr. Mahesh Chandra, representative of *Hindusthan Times*.

June 20, 1959. The Dalai Lama issues a statement in Mussoorie and at a Press conference he repudiates the Seventeen-Point Treaty and accuses the Chinese of attempting to destroy the Tibetan religion, culture and race.

June 30, 1959. A Government of India spokesman states that the Government did not recognise any separate Government of Tibet and there is no question of a Tibetan Government under the Dalai Lama functioning in India.

July 4, 1959. The Dalai Lama during an interview at Mussoorie states: that he would do nothing or make any pronouncements which might embarrass the Government of India to whom he was extremely grateful for having given him asylum; referring to a New China News Agency announcement that land re-distribution and other land reforms are being carried out after the rebellion had been crushed, he reaffirms that he would welcome any reforms in his land if they were in accordance with the religion and ancient structure of Tibetan society; 50,000 Tibetans are waging guerrilla warfare against the Chinese as late as a month ago; that as an ardent Buddhist he appealed to his people to stop fighting and bloodshed.